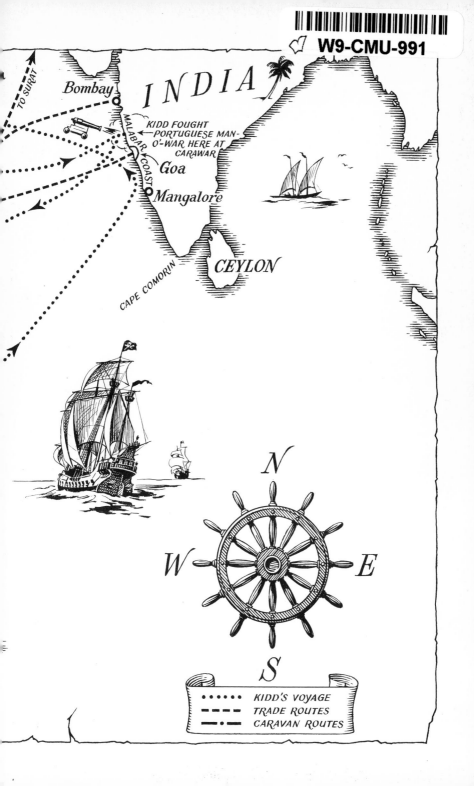

INDIA

Bombay

KIDD FOUGHT
PORTUGUESE MAN-
O'-WAR HERE AT
CARAWAR

MALABAR COAST

Goa

Mangalore

TO SURAT

CAPE COMORIN

CEYLON

N

W   E

S

•••••• KIDD'S VOYAGE
– – – TRADE ROUTES
–·–·– CARAVAN ROUTES

Freebooters of the
Red Sea

Pirates attacking a treasure ship. (From the painting by Howard Pyle.)

FREEBOOTERS OF THE RED SEA:

Pirates, Politicians and Pieces of Eight

by HAMILTON COCHRAN

THE BOBBS-MERRILL COMPANY, INC.

A Subsidiary of Howard W. Sams & Co., Inc.

Publishers · INDIANAPOLIS · KANSAS CITY · NEW YORK

The author wishes to thank Messrs. George Allen & Unwin, Ltd. for permission to quote passages from THE MEMOIRS OF A BUCCANEER, by Louis Le Golif. Translated by Malcolm Barnes. George Allen and Unwin, Ltd. London. 1961.

TO MY GRANDSONS
Robert Nixon Taylor, Jr.,
and
James Hamilton Taylor

ACKNOWLEDGMENTS

The author acknowledges with sincere thanks the friendly assistance of the following persons and organizations in supplying source material and illustrations for this book: Mr. Robert Nesmith of Foul Anchor Archives for making available copies of rare and unpublished documents. Mr. Bruce St. John, Director, The Wilmington Society of the Fine Arts, Delaware Art Center, Wilmington, Delaware, for permission to reproduce paintings and illustrations of pirates by the late Howard Pyle. Also to the Philadelphia Athenaeum, The New York Historical Society, and the Pennsylvania Historical Society for making their facilities available for research.

Contents

Illustrations

A Note on the Illustrations

No authentic portrait of Captain Kidd or any of the other pirates described in this book is known to exist. This is quite understandable in the light of their occupation. Consequently all the illustrations are the imaginative production of their creators.

THE AUTHOR

Introduction

ALTHOUGH the time span of this book covers scarcely fifteen years at the end of the seventeenth century, they were years of intense excitement, controversy, political chicanery and sudden riches. The period comprises a facet of history which, I believe, deserves greater attention, because it was the first time in the history of the American colonies that political corruption and the flouting of British law became widespread. The wealth so quickly amassed by public officials, merchants and shipowners of New York, Philadelphia, Providence and Boston came from one main source: the Red Sea Men. Veterans of the Spanish Main, they were pirates and freebooters who had deserted the Caribbean to prey on the richly laden ships of both the Great Mogul of India and the East India Company in the Red Sea and Indian Ocean.

Because the foreign trade of the American colonies was restricted by stringent Navigation Acts, the arrival of smuggled merchandise from the Orient—rich silks and satins, spices, gems and other luxury items—was as sensational as it was welcome. Merchants who had formerly conducted their affairs with rigid honesty yielded to the temptation to buy looted goods at a few shillings in the pound. Bribery, protection of criminals, and corruption of every sort eroded the integrity of public officials, from governors to customs officers.

Some of the most distinguished colonial families, including many Quakers, founded their fortunes on pirate booty from the Red Sea. The impact of the Red Sea Men on the economic, political and moral life of the American colonies was deep but temporary. It ended when an honest governor, supported by high officials of the British Crown, disrupted and finally ended the heyday of the Red Sea Men. Most of them died fighting or at the end of a rope. The most notorious, Captain William Kidd, hung in chains at Tilbury Point on the Thames, his sightless eyes the food for crows, as a warning to honest seamen not to follow in the wake of the Red Sea Men.

*Freebooters of the
Red Sea*

1

Piracy Was Big Business

From the very beginning of recorded history there have been armed men who preferred to steal from others rather than earn an honest living. Ashore they were called thieves, robbers or highwaymen. On the high seas they were called pirates.

The Mediterranean was the birthplace of piracy, for the richly laden merchant galleys of Greece and Rome offered tempting spoils to men bold enough to attack them. Hundreds of years later, the Vikings[1] prowled the narrow seas between the British Isles, Scandinavia and the mainland of Europe, raiding, plundering, and murdering as they went.

All through the Middle Ages, European and English merchants ran the risk of having their vessels attacked and captured by sea robbers, particularly along the coasts of Algeria and Tunis.

It was after the discovery of America by Christopher Columbus and the exploitation of the Spanish colonies that piracy developed into organized big business. Great galleons loaded with gold, silver, pearls and valuable raw materials from the New World sailed in convoy for Spain. Here was rich treasure ready for the taking, for the vessels had to pass through one of the straits between the West Indian islands before they were free of the land and could point toward Spain. It is impossible to estimate the value of booty taken by the pirates between 1500 and 1700, but it ran into the hundreds of millions of dollars. Nevertheless a tremendous quantity of riches reached Spain safely and made that country the most prosperous kingdom in the world.

Toward the last quarter of the seventeenth century, Spain strengthened its naval forces to such an extent that fewer and fewer treasure galleons were captured by the pirates. True, Henry Morgan, the buccaneer captain, had led a pirate army across the Isthmus of Panama and captured and burned the rich city of Panama, in 1671, escaping with millions in booty. But after Spain's loud and angry protests, it was open season on pirates of all sorts. Morgan himself was knighted by Charles II of England and sent back to Jamaica as Lieutenant Governor with strict orders to track down and destroy his former pirate cronies. This he did with such energy that for many years piracy was at a low ebb in the Caribbean.

In this situation the professional pirates cast their eyes elsewhere for loot. They found it thousands of miles eastward, in the Red Sea and the Indian Ocean.

At this time the Great Mogul of India ruled a vast Mohammedan empire. He commanded a large fleet of merchant vessels that plied the Bay of Bengal, the Arabian Sea, the Red Sea and the Persian Gulf. Active trade had been developed among the various native kingdoms bordering on those seas. Merchant vessels carried rich cargoes of silks, spices, gold dust, ivory, exotic perfumes, pearls, precious stones, muslins and rich cloths of gold and silver. Some of the merchandise, including spices and especially pepper, were destined for Red Sea ports. These cities were located at the beginning of the great caravan routes which crossed the Nubian Desert and followed the Nile to Cairo and Alexandria and ports of the eastern Mediterranean.

The Red Sea area, the pirates reasoned, offered booty beyond the dreams of avarice, with comparatively easy pickings. The Great Mogul, while developing his merchant marine, had neglected to organize an efficient navy. Until the advent of the Red Sea Men, there was little piracy in the area. It was largely practiced by small groups of men in fast sailing dhows or galleys. The Mogul's armed merchantmen had been able to survive most of their attacks.

But the Great Mogul was not the only fleet owner who plied these seas. There were also the British East India Company and the Portuguese and the Dutch. The English East India Company was founded at the end of the sixteenth century. Its purpose was to compete with Dutch merchants who had secured a practical monopoly of the rich trade with the Spice Islands. These shrewd Dutch traders had raised the price of pepper from three shillings to eight shillings a pound. Queen Elizabeth, refusing to pay exorbitant prices for spices, issued a royal charter December 31, 1600, under the title of "The Governor and Company of Merchants of London, Trading into the East Indies." This charter conferred on them the sole right of trading with the East Indies, that is, all countries lying east of the Cape of Good Hope and west of the Straits of Magellan. Unauthorized interlopers, if captured, were liable to forfeiture of ships and cargo.

Almost immediately friction arose between the English

East India Company and the Dutch East India Company. The Dutch traders felt that they had prior rights to the Far East, claiming that their hold on the Indian Archipelago had been firmly planted on the basis of domination and authority in those territories. Although there were short periods of peace, the competition for the spice trade continued.

The English East India Company early recognized the necessity for having stout ships and competent crews. The design of their sailing vessels not only permitted large cargoes, but enabled the ships to sail well before the wind. They were also well armed. They had to be prepared at any moment to fight—not merely Malay pirates, but the armed trading vessels of their Dutch, French and Portuguese rivals. Many battles were fought among these rival factions along the trade routes.

Now a new danger threatened—the arrival of Yankee pirates who had deserted the Caribbean. During the reign of Charles II, who granted the East India Company five important charters, the organization developed from a simple trading company to a great chartered organization with the right to acquire territory, coin money, command fortresses and troops, form alliances, make war and peace, and exercise both civil and criminal jurisdiction. The company prospered prodigiously.

Tall ships of the English East India Company steadily plied the Indian Ocean, carrying British manufactured goods to Oriental ports and returning home with precious cargoes of tea, coffee, spices and textiles.

It is somewhat surprising that the Yankee pirates did not hesitate to ply their trade in the face of the well-armed East India Company. But they only attacked these ships if they were storm-damaged or sailing without convoy. Much easier to pursue and capture were the somewhat smaller, ill-armed vessels belonging to the Great Mogul and local princes along the coast of the Red Sea, Arabia and India.

There was a vast amount of rich loot to be taken by resolute and desperate men. After these cargoes had been captured, where could they be disposed of? Gold and silver coin, gold dust, gold bars and silver were easy enough to trade with, for they were mediums of exchange in all countries. But what about the diamonds, rubies, emeralds and pearls which frequently formed part of the booty? Also the vast quantity of rich textiles, ivory, jade, and spices? Was there a market for these?

The answer was an emphatic *yes*. The markets for pirates' merchandise were not located in the Far East, but thousands of miles westward on the Atlantic coast of the American colonies. The merchants who bought these stolen goods were among the most respectable men in the American colonies. But more of that later.

Now let us take a look at the area in the Far East which was the cruising ground of the Red Sea Men.

Captain Roberts' crew carousing on the Malabar Coast after a successful raid on the ships of the Great Mogul. (From The Pirates' Own Book.)

2

Madagascar, Malabar and the Red Sea Trade

Pirates of the seventeenth and eighteenth centuries did not have much book learning. Many of them could not even read or write. But they were well versed in three primary matters necessary to their trade: fighting, seamanship and a knowledge of geography. These freebooters were bound into a sort of confraternity. They exchanged information relating to trade routes, coastal towns weakly defended and ripe for picking, also the cruising grounds of men-of-war that were searching for gallows bait such as themselves.

There were two principal locations in the Indian Ocean convenient to the southern part of the Red Sea which became the headquarters of many of the pirates operating in that area. One was the large island of Madagascar and its small tributary island of St. Mary (Ste. Marie). The other location was known as the Malabar Coast.

Madagascar is the fourth largest island in the world, exceeded in size only by Greenland, New Guinea and Borneo. It lies 260 miles east of the coast of Africa, from which it is separated by the Mozambique Channel. Madagascar is nearly 1000 miles in length from north to south and averages about 250 miles in breadth. Its area covers approximately 228,000 square miles, not quite four times the size of England and Wales. The center of the island is mountainous, with peaks ranging from 3000 to 5000 feet in altitude. Along the seacoast the land is fairly level and suitable for agriculture.

During the first half of the seventeenth century, the people of Madagascar were divided into a number of tribes, separated from each other by large areas of uninhabited land. In 1650 a small but warlike people called Sakalava conquered most of the other tribes and founded two kingdoms which retained their supremacy until the close of the eighteenth century.

The influence of the Arabs on Madagascar dates from very early times. They were traders and merchants. There also was a distinctive Hindu influence, for, again from earliest times, a flourishing trade had been maintained between India and northern Madagascar. Consequently there were a large number of merchant vessels plying between Red Sea ports and Madagascar and between the latter island and the Malabar Coast of India.

During the era of the pirates, cattle raising and the dressing of hides was one of the principal industries of the island. Timber and various precious woods were also exported. The island produced a variety of fruits and vegetables including yams, sweet potatoes, arrowroot, bananas, pineapples and mangoes. So there was no problem about food as far as the pirates were concerned.

And there was gold. This precious mineral was found almost everywhere throughout the island, being in the form of crystalline rocks. Silver and platinum were also produced in small quantities. All in all, Madagascar was an ideal headquarters for piratical men who needed provisions and a safe port from which to operate.

Twenty-four hundred miles northeast of Madagascar lay the great subcontinent of India. Its southwestern coast, known as the Western Ghats, stretched from Bombay to the Gulf of Mannar. This region was also known as the Malabar Coast. It consisted of low tablelands merging toward the coast into rice plains and backwaters fringed with coconut palms. The coast runs in a southeasterly direction and forms a few headlands and small bays with a natural harbor in the south at Cochin. One important characteristic of the Malabar Coast, and important to the pirates, was a continuous chain of lagoons lying parallel to the coast. Connected by artificial canals, they formed an easy means of transit. A large local trade was conducted on these inland waterways.

Here was a rich hunting ground for sea robbers, for an active import and export business was carried on between the ports of Bombay, Goa (then a Portuguese enclave), Mangalore, Calicut and other cities. So now we have the triangle of operation of the Red Sea Men. The apex of the triangle was the southern outlet of the Red Sea and the Gulf of Aden. The base of the triangle was formed by a line running between Madagascar and the Malabar Coast. It may seem surprising that American pirates cruised in such a vast area. Just to get there required a long passage around the Cape of Good Hope. But to hardened mariners, hungry for gold, distance was of little moment.

Captain Charles Johnson, who wrote the classic *A Gen-*

eral History of the Robberies and Murders of the Most Notorious Pirates (London, 1724), gives this description of the island of Madagascar:

> It abounds with provisions of all sorts, oxen, goats, sheep, poultry, fish, citrons, oranges, tamarinds, dates, coconut, bananas, wax, honey, rice or in short, cotton, indigo, or any thing they [the inhabitants] will take pains to plant and have understanding to manage. They have likewise ebony, a hard wood like brazil, of which they make their lances; and gum of all sorts, benzoin, dragon's blood, aloes and so forth. What is most incommodious are the numerous swarms of locusts on the land and crocodiles or alligators in the rivers. Hither, in St. Augustin's Bay, the ships sometimes touch for water, when they take the inner passage for India.

> Since the discovery of this island by the Portuguese, A.D. 1506, the Europeans, and particularly Pirates, have increased a dark mulatto race there, though still few in comparison with the natives, who are Negroes with curled short hair. They are active and were formerly represented as malicious and revengeful, but are now tractable and communicable, perhaps owing to the favors and generosity in clothing and liquors they, from time to time, have received from these fellows [pirates] who live in all possible friendship and can, any single man of them, command a guard of two or three hundred at a minute's warning ... Because the island [is] divided into petty governments and commands, the pirates settled here are now a considerable number and have little castles of their own.

Captain Johnson, who is suspected of having consorted with pirates himself, and very possibly may have taken part in piratical cruises, praises Madagascar for its abundant food supplies and cheap labor:

> This island of Madagascar affords all necessaries of life and yields to none, either in the wholesomeness of the air or the

fruitfulness of the soil. The seas around it are well stored with fish, the woods with fowl . . .

The soil will produce sugar, cotton, indigo, and other growths of our American colonies, at a far inferior expense; as I will make plain, by comparing the charge of erecting a mill and so forth in Barbadoes, with what it would be here.

A wind mill in Barbadoes will cost one hundred pounds, all materials and labor being very dear; but here, wood and stone may be had for labor only, so that with artificers, and the need for iron and copper work brought from Europe, a sugar work may be set up for very little money. Negroes in Barbadoes are [bought] at thirty pounds, forty pounds or fifty pounds per head, and I dare answer to ten shillings in European goods will purchase a Negro slave at Madagascar, since we have purchased for an old colt, a lusty fellow.

This appears to be rather good proof that Captain Johnson visited Madagascar and perhaps indulged in a little slave trading on his own account!

Food is very dear at Barbadoes and here [in] Madagascar you may feed a slave, as well as yourself without expense, consequently he will do more work than a Barbadoes slave, who is, by the dearness of provision, half starved.

It should be kept in mind that Johnson's statement of the expensiveness of food for slaves in Barbadoes is correct. New England merchant captains were the chief supply of slave food for the islands, bringing down salt codfish, and corn meal to trade for sugar, molasses and rum. The salt codfish and corn meal were boiled into a mess called "fungi," the staple diet of the slaves along with local fruits and vegetables. Fungi is still a favorite part of West Indian Negroes' diet.

But to proceed to other advantages: all sorts of medicinal and dyeing woods may be carried from hence [Madagascar] to Europe, and your woods for fine works, as ironwood, ceder, mahogany, and so forth are here in great abundance.

If a colony with a lawful power were settled here, no doubt that many of the commodities which we fetch from the Indies might be made here, as silk, cotton, and so forth, the soil being proper for their production.

The natives are, or seem to be, very humane and they have such plenty of black cattle, that we have bought an ox of 800 pounds weight for a pair of breeches.

Besides, a settlement here would be a curb on Pirates and a protection as well as a great conveniency to our East India ships, who might be stored with fresh or soft provisions and consequently not be obliged to carry with them so great a quantity as they now do, and save a great deal of money to the company in their victualling.

The adjacent island of St. Mary, lying only a few miles off the northeast coast, was also a strategic haven for the pirates. It, too, had many advantages for defense against attack. Soon the word spread that St. Mary was ideal as a base for looting Moslem ships plying between India and the Red Sea.

It is not often that history provides a firsthand account of a pirate expedition. Fortunately a certain Samuel Perkins from Ipswich, in Massachusetts Bay Colony, who had been kidnaped by pirates, made a deposition to the English government on August 25, 1698. Here is his story:

In the year 1693, Perkins, a landsman, went aboard the *Resolution* commanded by Captain Robert Glover. Perkins's purpose was to visit his uncle Elisha Skilling, the boatswain of the *Resolution*. Apparently his uncle had very little family feeling, for he locked up the youth and prevented him from going ashore as the ship got under weigh for parts unknown.

As soon as the coast of North America had sunk below the horizon, Captain Glover hoisted the skull and crossbones to the masthead and declared that all hands were going a-roving. After rounding the Cape of Good Hope, the *Resolution* anchored at a port in Madagascar. From there they sailed north into the Red Sea to await a large convoy of merchantmen from India.

But luck was not with the would-be pirates. The ships from India did not show up. Provisions and water running low, they ran for the island of Socotra east of the Gulf of Aden.

After obtaining food and water there, their course was typical of cruises made by other tough Yankee seamen who had taken up piracy. From the island of Socotra the *Resolution* sailed clear across the Indian Ocean to the port of Rajapur in India, located somewhat south of the great city of Bombay. Here they intercepted a small armed vessel from Muscat mounting twelve guns and carrying dates and rice. Somewhere between Madagascar and the Malabar Coast, Captain Glover had been replaced by Richard Shivers, who pointed the vessel to Mangalore and captured another Muscat ship. Then they sailed down the Malabar Coast to Calicut Road where four Moslem ships fell into their clutches. When they had reached the very tip end of India near Cape Comorin, they captured a Danish vessel which gave them sorely needed guns and ammunition and also furnished additional crew members. For these unfortunate Danes, it was death unless they joined the pirates, which they did. Turning westward, they put in to the island of Mauritius. Here they again provisioned and sailed for St. Mary Island which had been their original goal.

At anchor in the harbor of St. Mary was another Yankee ship, the *John and Rebecca* of two hundred tons and fourteen guns, hailing from Rhode Island. This ship had been supplied and provisioned by a Rhode Island merchant. He had concealed his identity so well that in testifying before the English court, Perkins was unable to give his name. At the time of the arrival of the *Resolution*, the crew of the *John and Rebecca* were having a great celebration, drinking, feasting, and dancing with the St. Mary girls. Their carousing was in celebration of their capture in the Gulf of Persia of a great ship, richly laden with merchandise belonging to a merchant of Surat. Another ship in the harbor at this time was out of New York, sent there by the good merchants of that city to purchase Negro slaves.

In addition to the two American vessels there was the frigate *Mocha*, formerly an East Indiaman which had been stolen by the pirates and converted for their use. Also the *Charles and Mary*, an English vessel, and a number of other ships whose pirate crews were English or European.

As the result of Perkins's deposition, it was to be expected that the British government would make a real attempt to rout out this nest of freebooters. Surprisingly, it was only a weak and largely unsuccessful gesture. Captain Warren of the Royal Navy sailed down to St. Mary with a boxful of pardons from the king, to be handed out on the promise that the pirates would quit their evil ways and settle down to honest work. Only a few of the rovers submitted. The rest merely shrugged and continued their robberies and carousing.

Soon the pickings in the Red Sea and Indian Ocean became so great that practically every Anglo-American pirate worthy of the name sailed to this part of the world. Some made St. Mary their home port. Others settled and fortified key points along the coast of Madagascar.

Captain John Avery and his pirate vessel capturing a ship of the Great Mogul. (From an old print.)

3

Captain John Avery,
Red Sea Champion

THE man most responsible for spreading the word about rich booty to be taken in the Red Sea and the Indian Ocean was Captain John Avery. It was he who virtually discovered and recognized this happy hunting ground among Indian merchantmen and ships belonging to the Great Mogul. As Columbus discovered the New World, so John Avery discovered a new world of easy loot, a safe harbor at St. Mary and a shore position that could easily be fortified. Such a combination was irresistible and John Avery made the most of it.

As Captain Charles Johnson aptly wrote a few years after Avery's death: "None of these bold adventurers were ever so much talked of for awhile, as Avery; he made a great noise in the world . . . and was looked upon to be a person of great consequence; he was represented in Europe as one that had raised himself to the dignity of a king and was likely to be the founder of a new monarchy, having taken immense riches."

Avery became so famous in England that a play, *The Successful Pirate*, was written about him. The work of none other than Captain Charles Johnson, it was produced at Drury Lane Theatre in November 1712. The scene is Madagascar and the character of the pirate king, Arviragus, is based upon Avery himself. A contemporary critic, Dennis, severely criticized the play and particularly the author for "Making a tarpaulin and a swabber . . . the Hero of a Tragedy." Avery's career also captured the imagination of Daniel Defoe, who took him for his hero in his *Life, Adventures and Piracies of Captain Singleton.*

John Avery (or "Long Ben," as he was commonly called) was born near Plymouth in Devonshire, England. He went to sea at an early age and served as a mate aboard a merchantman in which he made several voyages to the West Indies. At this time piracy was a popular trade among these islands, for the Spanish plate fleet was still making its semiannual voyage, heavily laden with gems, precious metals and other rare cargoes from the New World.

In 1697 the Peace of Ryswick had been signed, establishing an alliance between Spain, England and Holland against France. Nevertheless the French settlers on Martinique engaged in a very profitable smuggling trade with the Spaniards on the east coast of South America. Since the laws of Spain prohibited anyone but native Spaniards from engaging in trade with their colonies, smuggling became a popular and profitable pastime. The transition from smuggler to pirate was a very slight and painless one and many crossed the line.

In an effort to suppress the smuggling trade, the Spanish kept several ships cruising along the coast of their colonies.

These were called *Guardas Costas* and were under orders to make prizes of all ships found within five leagues (fifteen miles) of the coast of New Spain.

The *Guardas Costas* were small vessels and were usually routed by the Spanish smugglers. These had now become so strong that the Spanish government, being limited as to ships for *Guardas Costas* work, resolved to hire two or three large, stout foreign ships for this service. When this news reached the ever alert merchants of Bristol, England, they provided two sturdy vessels mounting thirty guns and carrying 120 hands each. These were provisioned and armed by the same merchants, who well appreciated the handsome profits they would make from the merchandise captured from the smugglers.

Presently the two English *Guardas Costas* sailed for La Coruña in Spain and there received their orders. At the same time a number of Spanish gentlemen came aboard as passengers to New Spain.

One of the English ships was named *The Duke* and its commander was one Captain Gibson. John Avery was signed on as first mate.

According to Johnson, Avery was "A fellow of more cunning than courage," and he insinuated himself into the good graces of several of the boldest seamen on board the other English ship as well as his own. "Having sounded their inclinations before he opened himself, and finding them right for his design, he at length proposed them to run away with the ship, telling them what great wealth was to be had upon the coast of India. It was no sooner said than agreed to, to execute their plot at ten o'clock the night following."

Avery's tall tales of the happy hunting ground in the Indian Ocean were not based on firsthand experience. He had never been there himself. But among the grogships of England's south coast and the rum-soaked *tavernas* of the West Indies, Avery had undoubtedly picked up some exciting yarns from Red Sea Men who had scouted the waters.

Now it happened that Captain Gibson was an alcoholic. (In those days such a man was referred to as "mighty addicted to punch.") Captain Gibson spent most of his time on shore, guzzling a powerful drink made from aged Spanish brandy.

Just as Avery was about to spring his plot, Captain Gibson, contrary to his usual custom, did not go ashore to drink, but remained on board.

Peeking around the cabin door, Avery was relieved to see that Captain Gibson was engaged in shipboard tippling. He kept it up most of the day and by dusk was dead drunk in his bunk. This suited the mutineers exactly. As Captain Gibson had conveniently passed out, now was the time for the plot to be sprung. Meanwhile the members of the crew who had not been invited to join the mutiny were snoring in their hammocks. To play safe, Avery had arranged that the watch on deck was to be composed exclusively of *his* men.

Avery had been busy conspiring not only aboard *The Duke* but also ashore. By prearrangement he went to the beach in the longboat, stopped briefly at several taverns and collected sixteen fellows who had agreed to enlist under Avery's black flag. Pushing out from shore they approached *The Duke* and hailed her.

"Is your drunken boatswain on board?" called Avery from the darkness.

"Aye," came the answer.

In a low voice Avery ordered the longboat alongside, for this exchange had been agreed upon as a signal that all was well aboard and that the besotted Gibson was still safely in his cabin.

"Lively now, my lads," whispered Avery. "Let's get *The Duke* under weigh."

No sooner said than done. The yards were braced, the sails set, and with a favoring breeze *The Duke* sailed boldly out of the harbor of Coruña, into the open seas. Although there was a Dutch frigate of forty guns in the harbor at the time, all was silent aboard.

Meanwhile Captain Gibson was not enjoying his usual heavy sleep. In the dark recesses of his alcoholic brain there was a seaman's awareness of strange sounds and motions. They were not those of a vessel peacefully at anchor. Drowsily he heard the trample of feet overhead, the creak of cables and cordage and the rhythmic motion of a ship under weigh. He raised his elbow and groggily rang his bell for the steward, demanding to see his first mate, Avery, at once.

"What is the matter?" the captain demanded.

Avery answered coolly, "Nothing."

The captain replied, "Something's the matter with the ship. Does she drive? What weather is it?"

In his befuddled mind he thought that a tempest had arisen in the harbor and that his reliable Avery had put to sea to ride out the storm.

Avery assured him that this was not the case. "No, no," he explained, "don't be in a fright, but put on your clothes and I'll let you into the secret. You must know, that I am captain of this ship now, and this is my cabin, and therefore you must walk out. I am bound to Madagascar, for the design of making my own fortune, and that of all the brave fellows joined in with me."

Never in his life had Captain Gibson sobered so quickly. His eyes were wide with fright. Avery, smiling into the man's pale, puffy face, remarked, "You have nothing to fear, Captain. If you have a mind to make one of us we will receive you; and if you will turn sober and mind your business, perhaps in time I may make you one of my lieutenants. If not there is a boat alongside and you shall be set ashore."[1]

To give the rogue his due, Avery was at least merciful to his former skipper, as was Fletcher Christian to Captain Bligh at the time of the mutiny of the *Bounty*. In contrast, many a mutineer had butchered the captain and loyal crew and tossed their bodies overboard. It was, they claimed, quick and more convenient, with less waste of words.

Captain Gibson took less than a split second to make up his mind to quit the ship. Whereupon the new captain mustered the crew on the quarterdeck and demanded to know who was willing to go on shore with the captain or who would seek their fortunes in Madagascar and the Red Sea. To Gibson's astonishment and Avery's satisfaction, only five or six of those who had not been let in on the plot decided to go ashore with Gibson.

Since the vessel was only a few leagues offshore, Avery allowed the captain and his men to go in peace, amply provided with water and provisions. Then the yards were braced, the tiller put hard over and *The Duke's* bowsprit pointed for the Cape of Good Hope.

The pirates reached Madagascar after an uneventful voyage. When they arrived at the northeast part of the island they noticed two sloops anchored in a small bay. In panic, the sloops' crews slipped cables and ran their vessels ashore; then they ran into the woods and hid themselves.

Avery called to them not to be afraid. They came out of hiding and proved to be the crews of two boats which had been stolen in the West Indies. The men had fled to the woods in their fear that Avery's larger ship was a government frigate sent to capture them. They were well armed and overjoyed to find that Avery and his men were pirates like themselves.

After due consultation with his new friends, Avery decided to go cruising with his vessel and the other two. So all hands turned to, hauled the sloops off the beach and sailed for the Arabian Sea.

As they neared the mouth of the River Indus, the lookout at the masthead shouted the welcome cry, "Sail ho!" Now, at last, it looked as if there would be action.

Upon closer approach, the quarry appeared to be a tall ship, possibly a Dutch East Indiaman, homeward bound. But when the vessel hoisted the colors of the Great Mogul they knew they really had a rich prize in view. She was called the *Gunsway*. The Mogul's ship placed itself in a position of defense, and the cautious Avery thought best to stand off and exchange broadsides at a respectable distance.

This plan of action did not suit most of his crew, for many of them were veteran buccaneers who had captured ships by boarding, with cutlass, pistol and pike. There was grumbling among the gun crews that Captain Avery was not so desperate a character as he claimed. Otherwise he would board the Mogul's ship without delay.

Meanwhile the two sloops had come up and, in true buccaneer fashion, clapped the Mogul on board and swarmed over the bulwarks shouting yells and curses, and discharging their pistols in the faces of the startled Hindus. They had scarcely reached the quarterdeck when down came the Mogul's flag and the ship surrendered.

After Avery and the rest of the crew had hurried on board, they were amazed at the richness of the captured vessel. It was truly one of the proud ships of the Great Mogul, carrying distinguished passengers and members of his court. On questioning, these people said that the ship was en route to the Red Sea on a pilgrimage to Mecca. The most notable person on board was the daughter of the Great

Mogul himself. With her was a retinue of fair maidens, and there were gold, silver, frankincense, rare spices and precious jewels to offer at the shrine of Mohamet. There is a legend that Avery was so smitten with the Mogul's daughter that he married her and settled her in Oriental splendor in a "castle" on St. Mary Island.

Although Avery and his men were awed at the lavishness of the vessel and its cargo, it was nothing out of the ordinary, for it was the usual practice for Oriental people to travel in utmost magnificence. In rummaging through the ship, Avery's crew found a number of household slaves, as well as rich clothing and jewels, vessels of gold and silver, and great sums of money to pay the expenses of the long journey to Mecca.

No reliable estimate survives of the value of the booty. But it must have amounted to several million dollars. One account states that Avery took 100,000 pieces of eight and an equal number of sequins (Turkish gold coins worth about $2.50).

Avery promptly plundered the ship of everything valuable, including provisions, gear of all types, cannon, powder and shot. He then allowed the vessel to proceed, mercifully sparing the passengers and crew from the usual procedure of slitting throats and throwing captives overboard.

When the news of the looting of the Mogul's ship reached that grand monarch, he burned with rage. He especially hated the English and threatened dire reprisals against their settlements on the Indian coast. This was not at all to the liking of the English East India Company which was engaging in a flourishing mercantile trade in that part of the world. There were long faces in the Board Room of the East India Company when the news reached London, and the matter received great publicity in the English newspapers. That is probably one reason why Avery and his crew received more than they deserved in the way of notoriety.

In evaluation of his exploit, it seems very possible that Avery would have refused to clap the Mogul's ship aboard had it not been for the tough buccaneers of the two sloops who swarmed over her shortly after Avery had softened up the enemy with his cannon. Contrary to the usual situation, there was little if any bloodshed aboard the Mogul's ship. It was a merchant vessel and not a man-of-war. Consequently the captain, officers and crew were not particularly good fighting men, and Indians were known to give in rather easily.

Afterwards, Avery and his crew sailed back to Madagascar, full of plans to settle on the island, fortify their lair, and, leaving a small garrison, set out in search of further booty.

But before reaching the island of refuge, shrewd Avery invited the captains of the two sloops aboard his vessel to hold a council regarding a division of loot. Avery apparently was a smooth and persuasive talker. He had a plan, he said, that would virtually guarantee the safety of the booty against accidents until arrival at Madagascar. He pointed out that the treasure was worth nothing unless it was safely put ashore and fairly divided. The greatest danger, he declared, was from capture by other and stronger pirates. Therefore, Avery said, it would be the height of wisdom for all of the treasure to be placed aboard his own large and well-armed vessel.

"Consider the consequences of being separated by bad weather," he reasoned. "If either of your vessels should fall in with any ships of force and either be taken or sunk, your treasure on board would be lost. Also you should not forget the ordinary hazards of storm and stress of weather.

"As for my part," he continued, "my vessel is strong and able to make defense against any ship we are likely to meet in these seas. If I meet with any ship of such strength that I cannot take her, I am safe from being taken, being so well manned. Besides, my ship is quick and can carry sail when your sloops cannot.

"Seal up each chest with three seals, whereof each of us will keep one. Then we will appoint a rendezvous in case of separation."

The captains of the sloops, being members of the Brethren of the Coast (a buccaneer organization of Tortuga in the Caribbean), had always worked on this same basis of "One for all and all for one." True to the "code of honor among thieves," they had been used to sharing alike and had always trusted their leaders. So it is not surprising that the two captains, believing implicitly in Avery's word, deposited their loot aboard his vessel.

The three ships kept company for two or three days in fair weather. During this time the slippery Captain Avery focused his persuasive powers upon his own crew. He told them that with the great amount of treasure on board, each man was rich. He would have plenty to take care of himself for the rest of his life. Why not, therefore, slip away from the other two sloops and go to some country where they weren't known and live a life of ease and comfort ashore?

Avery's own men, being largely merchant seamen and not brought up in the strict precepts of the Brothers of the Coast, readily agreed to his proposition.

Remarks Captain Charles Johnson: "Nor do I find that any of them felt any qualms of honor rising in his stomach to hinder them from consenting to this piece of treachery. In fine, they took advantage of the darkness at night, steered another course, and by morning lost sight of them.

"I leave the reader to judge what swearing and confusion [there was] among the sloops' men when they saw that Avery had given them the slip. For they knew by the fairness of the weather and the course they had agreed to steer, that it must have been done on purpose."

As Avery's vessel proceeded pleasantly on its way, the question arose as to where to go with the spoils. It would be unwise, they realized, to proceed to Madagascar or any of the other pirate strongholds on the borders of the Indian Ocean or Red Sea, for it was quite certain that the Great Mogul would track them down and destroy them if he could. Nor would it be wise to sneak into some English port, since *The Duke* was of English registry and the news of the looting of the Great Mogul was bound to create a sensation in mercantile circles throughout the British Isles.

"America," Avery declared, "is the place for us, my lads. None of them knows us in those parts. There we can divide the treasure, change our names and go ashore; some in one place, some in another. We could each buy ourselves a town if we chose and live at our ease."

In answer, a great shout of approval arose from the crew. The tiller was put hard over and the vessel pointed toward the Western Ocean. The first landfall they made was the island of New Providence in the Bahamas. This had only recently been settled, but was a good place to anchor temporarily, for it was a favorite hideout of pirates of the Caribbean.

But before steering for the coast of America there were certain other serious things to consider, Avery realized. He reckoned that if he were to go to New England in the ship he now commanded it would cause something of a sensation, for vessels of that size bearing strange names were rare. Questions would be asked. It was quite possible also that Englishmen who had heard of Avery's mutiny and capture of the ship would recognize it and report him to Crown authorities as a pirate. So Avery thought it the better part of wisdom to get rid of the ship.

On arrival at New Providence Island, Avery again employed his lying and persuasive tongue. He let it be known that his vessel had been cruising as a privateer. As it had not met with any success, his owners had instructed him to sell the ship. He soon found a buyer who gave him a good price for it. With part of the money Avery purchased a sloop and with his crew headed for the American coast.

It is not certain where they first landed, but it is known that some came ashore on the coast of the Carolinas. Others slipped to the beach at Cape May, New Jersey. They passed themselves off as honest privateersmen and at this particular time, which was early in the era of the Red Sea Men, nothing much was made of it.

Most of Avery's share of the loot consisted of a large quantity of beautiful cut diamonds. It is likely that he concealed them from the rest of the crew, since there was no sign of them when the booty was being assembled. Avery's problem now was to transform those precious stones into gold and silver coinage of the realm.

We next hear of Avery in Boston where he landed with a few companions, and was said to have given the governor a handsome bribe for not molesting him. Nevertheless, he had cause to worry. Although he posed as an honest privateer who had made some fortunate captures, he did not dare to show his diamonds or try to sell them for fear that they would be quickly associated with the capture of the Great Mogul's ship. Diamonds were few in the American colonies. Besides, what merchant in Boston was wealthy enough to pay Avery a fraction of the value of this great store of precious gems? Avery also realized that because of the prevalence of piracy throughout the West Indies and along the North American coast, anyone suspected of being a pirate could be seized and jailed until he could prove his innocence at a London trial.

With these thoughts in mind, Avery persuaded his men to join him on a voyage to Ireland. Somewhere on the north coast they separated. Avery sold the sloop and settled for a while in one of the northern Irish cities.

Meanwhile, news of Avery's capture of the Mogul's vessel had spread far and wide: from Boston south along the Atlantic coast, down through Cuba, clear to the Spanish Main. Fired with prospects of quick and easy wealth, hundreds of rovers set sail for the Red Sea.

Although John Avery may have been a swashbuckling captain on the quarterdeck of his own vessel and a shrewd man with ignorant pirates, he was a fearful and credulous person ashore. He was still greatly bothered about those diamonds and wanted to get rid of them. After much thought he decided to go across from Ireland to Bristol, a thriving seaport, and try and dispose of them there. He was afraid to go directly to the gem merchants, so he used an intermediary, a man he could trust, from the town of Bideford. Avery reasoned that Bristol merchants, being men of wealth and credit in the world, would not ask embarrassing questions about the origin of the diamonds, particularly if they were offered at an unusually attractive price. Avery's friend assured him that he was on very intimate terms with some of these merchants who had connections all over Europe and would undoubtedly dispose of the diamonds in no time at all. Avery was pleased with this plan.

Shortly after Avery's friend had traveled from Bideford to Bristol to consult with the merchants, they visited Avery, looked over the diamonds and declared them of excellent quality. Avery concealed his identity and the source of the gems. They told him that the value of the diamonds was so great that they could not consider outright purchase, but would sell them for him on commission. Disappointed, but deciding that this was the best he could do, Avery accepted their terms. They paid him a small amount as a token of good faith and went off with the diamonds.

Then Avery settled down in Bideford, still living under an assumed name. The people paid little attention to him, for he did not throw his money about or talk loudly in the taverns.

When Avery had spent all the money the merchants had given him and still had not heard anything from them, he began to be uneasy. He wrote them letter after letter without receiving any reply. At last they sent him another small supply of money which was scarcely sufficient to pay his debts.

Finally he became so desperate for money, even enough to keep alive, that he journeyed to Bristol to demand full payment for his diamonds. Here he met a most shocking repulse. When he demanded that the merchants settle with him, they told him to keep quiet or they would expose him to the authorities as a pirate—the man who robbed the Great Mogul. Once unmasked, he would promptly be clapped in jail, tried, and probably hanged.

Greatly shaken and undecided what to do next, Avery slunk off to Ireland and from there kept pestering the merchants without success. His money now entirely gone, the once proud pirate captain was reduced to beggary. As a last desperate measure Avery returned to England. He was so poor that he could not even pay his fare on a coach but walked on foot from Plymouth to Bideford. The exposure and worry so told on his health that he took sick and died, "not being worth as much as would buy him a coffin."

Pirates who silently boarded a treasure ship at night surprised the captain in his cabin while playing cards. (From an illustration by Howard Pyle.)

4

Pirate Empire

DURING the decade following Captain John Avery's great haul, the Isle of St. Mary and the bays and coves of the coast of Madagascar were settled and fortified by a new influx of American, English, and French pirates who flocked to the area, hoping to equal Avery's masterpiece.

The harbor of St. Mary was large enough to accommodate at least a dozen large ships. There was plenty of free labor to construct fortifications for protection of the port, for the freebooters had captured and enslaved many black people. The pirates also provided themselves with an ample number of concubines from among the dark-skinned natives, choosing young girls between the ages of fourteen and eighteen.

Several of the leaders built "castles" like the one John Avery was said to have lived in. These "castles" were merely fortified houses, protected by wooden palisades and a number of cannon. It is unlikely that the dwellings were elaborate.[1]

The men of St. Mary were true pirates as distinct from privateersmen. A privateersman was a member of the crew of a privately owned vessel, financed, provisioned and armed by private means. This vessel operated under a letter of marque provided by a governor or other responsible government official, authorizing the captain of the vessel to prey upon the enemies of that nation. Privateering was a long-established custom when pirates settled on St. Mary. But since the peace between France, Spain, Holland and England had been sealed by the Treaty of Ryswick in 1697, seamen and officers who had once served aboard privateers quickly shifted to careers of piracy. The only real difference between a privateer and a pirate was that the privateer preyed only on his country's enemies. But to a pirate, all nations, including his own, were fair game.

Neither the American nor English nor French pirates headquartered at St. Mary had any qualms about attacking vessels of the English East India Company if opportunity offered. Some of these ships were poorly manned by jail-birds or landsmen who could scarcely be counted on to put up a stiff fight. On an outward-bound voyage an East India-man would be loaded with manufactured goods of all sorts, including precious gunpowder, shot and perhaps even cannon and cannon balls for the defense of East India enclaves on the Malabar Coast. On the return voyage to England the same vessel would carry a valuable cargo of silks, muslins, ivory, spices, sandalwood and other exotic products of the Far East. Regardless of which way the vessel was headed, it would prove a valuable prize for the pirates. After the capture, the American pirates would sail for the colonies, there to exchange their loot for provisions, arms and other necessities.

To keep their hand in the business of killing during intervals between pirate voyages, the freebooters would take part in wars between local chieftains on the mainland of Madagascar. This resulted in additional slaves and the good will of their native allies.

The pirates treated the natives abominably. Although they aided them from time to time in the various cattle wars going on between native kings and chieftains, the common people suffered brutal exploitation, thievery and massacre.

Most of the pirates, being ignorant criminals who found themselves suddenly rich at the expense of Indian princes, fancied themselves Oriental potentates. They dressed in colorful costumes, and loaded themselves and their women with jewelry. They bargained and quarreled for the most beautiful young girls, maintained large harems, and vied with each other on the beauty of their inmates.

Although the pirates had fortified their hideouts by building log forts, protected by palisades and moats, they had an "escape hatch" in case they were overwhelmed by revengeful landing parties of the English or Dutch East India Companies. Their escape was through the jungle. It was deep and dark and crisscrossed with many paths known only to the pirates and their retinues. If the forts fell to the enemy, there was a good chance of escape into the interior of the island.

One of the most extensive pirate estates was that of John Pro.[2] He had made his wealth from operating out of St. Mary, but decided to settle on Madagascar where he owned large herds of cattle. His house was as big as an English mansion, but roughly constructed. It contained many of the luxuries and refinements typical of the home of an English country gentleman, including pewter dishes and canopied beds, but no chairs. Everyone sat on the floor, Oriental fashion. Chests were used for storing clothes and other possessions after the manner of the seventeenth century. There were many outbuildings, including a cookhouse, slaves' quarters, storehouses, and barns and corrals for the livestock.

An inspection of the defenses of St. Mary would have revealed a fort constructed of logs and sod, protected by twenty-one guns, well camouflaged by foliage. In front of the fort was a high stockade of pointed logs. Along the shore was a row of warehouses for the accommodation of the cargoes captured by the pirates. Inside were great bolts of East Indian muslin, calico, silks, and cloth of gold and silver and other merchandise waiting to be shipped to the American colonies or sold to any visiting merchant who would pay what was asked. At other times, lively trading took place for tobacco, firearms, powder, shot, provisions and all sorts of material the pirates needed for the maintenance and operation of their vessels.

The wharf where the cargoes were landed was known as "Shelley's Landing." It was named for Giles Shelley, an American pirate-trader, who often visited St. Mary and who was respected by the pirates.

Anchored peacefully in the bay were usually to be seen a variety of pirate craft and merchant vessels. The pirate ships varied greatly in size and armament. They ranged from small sloops to schooners, brigs and frigates. Often a young pirate would start out with only a small sloop. Gradually, through capture, he would acquire larger and larger vessels until he found one of a size to engage the biggest of the Great Mogul's ships or those of one of the East India companies.

As one pirate recorded in his memoirs: "It can be well imagined that I would have preferred a good brig, but everything has to begin at the beginning, and he who has a knife can, if he knows how to use it, procure a sword, and he who has a sword can procure cannon, provided he has daring and courage too."

Almost invariably the pirate craft was smaller than its prey. Yet it had the advantage of speed and audacity. It was not often that a pirate vessel would willingly attack a man-of-war. There would be little loot of value except cannon and ammunition. Moreover, the pirates would have to fight professional sailors who knew how to handle guns and fight hand-to-hand.

The tactics employed by the pirates varied according to time and place and the strategy of the pirate captain. Sometimes the pirates would dress themselves in native costumes and pretend to be Moslems on a pilgrimage to Mecca, lulling their prey into the belief that they were being approached by a friendly vessel. At other times the pirate ship would hang on the flanks of a convoy, waiting for some vessel to drop behind. It would then be pounced upon. Very rarely would a pirate vessel run parallel to an English or Dutch ship and exchange broadsides, for the merchantmen usually outgunned the pirate. On the other hand, many of the Great Mogul's merchant vessels and other Indian or Arabian ships carried cannon of small caliber which were ineffective against the heavier weight of metal aboard the pirate ship. Sometimes a merchant vessel, particularly if it was from India, would surrender after firing only a few token shots. But if the vessel was from England, Spain, France, Holland or Portugal, a much stiffer fight could be expected and victory would have to be gained by boarding.

Here is a description of the pursuit of a large merchant

vessel as recorded in Le Golif's memoirs.[3] Although this pursuit took place in the Caribbean, it is typical of the methods used by pirates of the seven seas.

The pirate vessel had been hanging on the heels of a large convoy, when a severe storm whipped out of the west. The vessels were scattered and next morning the pirates were overjoyed to see a large galleon wallowing along under jury rig, for the storm had broken two of her three great masts:

She was a very tall ship and almost as unrigged as a hulk. We soon saw that only her lower foremast remained, and on it they had set a cross jack and she was crawling along like a wounded lion. Since she could be none other than a Royal Spanish galleon, I imagine that the grumblings of a little while before would soon be drowned in cries of joy, and I at once made preparation for a fight.

In three hours we were astern of her at an angle to her horizon where her cannon, big as they were, could do no harm, being placed, as on all ships, on her two sides. Propelled only by a duster [a small sail] forward, she was greatly hindered from coming quickly into the wind to fire her broadside at us. Nevertheless she tried to do so, but with such slowness that I had no difficulty in remaining at her stern . . . In their condition they would have done better to have looked on us rather as rescuers than as enemies, and without delay to have struck the great Castillian ensign that flew from her castle, which was a veritable mountain of balusters, balconies and saints in painted wood, the whole surmounted by three very high lanterns and a great gilded crucifix.

One can imagine that, confident in the number of infantry soldiers they had on board, they thought they need not fear being taken by assault, and when they saw us within range they fired two rounds of cannon fire upon us through the stern ports even though I had not myself hoisted a flag. Having swung a little sideways, they were much too unsteady to be able to adjust their aim and their balls vanished in the waves under our lee. I then unfurled the filibuster [freebooter] flag and approached boldly.

Before this I had sent forward all the guns [muskets] I had on board, numbering ninety-three . . . I placed the best twelve of my adventurers in the ship's head above the beak-head frame with the order to fire on every living thing they could see . . . Each had behind him two of our men as servants, one to take away the empty gun and the other to pass him a loaded gun at once. And under my foresail I placed twenty more with the sole task of reloading the guns.

The men on the galleon sent us two more balls by their starboard ports, one of which made a great hole in our fore-sail, but they had not the time to reload and replace them, for we had meanwhile drawn very close and each of those who had been employed in serving these cannon quickly received a ball in the head or body. It will be understood that I was not considering boarding them at once. My plan was to be patient and remain behind them as long as was necessary to tire them and wear down their courage. We stayed in their wake until evening and sometimes so close that I had to swerve so as not to shatter my bowsprit on their poop. My men took advantage of this by firing their guns into the windows of the [galleon's] castle, where our balls broke the last panes spared by the storm, and they brought death into the main cabin, between the decks and in their batteries, which they enfiladed. The enemy persisted in using their stern-frame cannon, but each time they tried to do so, we killed so many that they had to give up. Nevertheless, before the sun sank we saw a strong body of soldiers show up to reply to us with their muskets; but the greater number were accounted for before they fired and the others, in order to get under cover as quickly as possi-ble, discharged their weapons without taking time to aim them, so they did us no harm.

When evening came they were all hidden and not a man showed himself on the galleon, which appeared to sail the waves without a living crew.

. . . At dawn I saw the galleon a short league to the north.

They had tried to change course in order to escape us, but in vain, because they could make no more progress than an old hulk, even though they had profited by the darkness to set up two jury-masts . . .

I soon caught up with them, but not without coming twice under the fire of their stern cannon. I placed myself once more in their wake and resumed the business with the guns. All day these poor people sailed with death behind them. They now hid themselves like rats. No longer seeing anything to fire upon, my men diverted themselves by cutting cables, rigging and ropes with their balls, and with cutting loose the pulleys and breaking them. They were so successful that an hour before sunset the masting they had put on the mizzen fell to port, and soon it was their main forward yardarm which collapsed with a great uproar on their forecastle, so that the ship was then no more than a great basket. I withdrew again before it was dark, but beforehand I twice came athwart and fired my two broadsides into their poop at short range, and we could see, when we came out of the smoke, that our [cannon] balls had shattered their helm. They also did great havoc among the [carved] saints that crowded around their castle, some of which had lost their heads and others their arms, while their great ensign was no more than a rag. In the early morning we saw that they had been able to make a few repairs to their rigging during darkness, and had striven to haul off to the west with the wind in their stern, which was all they could do. I had no more difficulty than the day before in rejoining them and, sailing into the wind, I sent into their wretched jury-masting a fine broadside of chain-ball which brought everything down again and in one instant destroyed the whole of their night's work. I then prepared to resume the business with the guns. I was ready to remain stuck to their stern for weeks and months if that should be necessary and until they gave up. But I had not to wait so long.

A little before noon they had had enough and struck their tattered ensign.

The sea had fallen enough for me to put out a boat, and go

aboard with a prize crew to receive the sword of the commander. There was no need to fear treachery, because the chief officers on these galleons were all of high rank and sometimes of the highest nobility, with an infinity of quarters on their escutcheons. [Here the narrator refers to their coats-of-arms, the number of quarterings indicating their noble lineage.] They were so infatuated with the idea of honor that they preferred to perish rather than once neglect its laws. And what I have said here of the Spanish officers of high rank is true of all officers of high rank in all Royal Navies on the sea.

I was received at the top of the ladder by an old and most venerable man, dressed all in black, with pleated ruffs, close-cropped head and a fine pointed grey beard. He introduced himself as having command of this galleon for the King. At his side was a smaller man in ecclesiastical robes and surrounded by four priests or friars. He informed me that he was Apostolic Vicar. He was on his way back to Aragón, his native land, in order to go from thence to Rome and report to his holiness the Pope concerning the mission which the latter had entrusted to him in the Americas and which was now ended. I asked his blessing, which he willingly gave me and which I received on my knees. . . . The old man [the commander] surrendered his sword, but I gave it back to him, wishing thereby to give evidence of my esteem for the fine defense he had put up. Plucking up courage after this, he told me most civilly that he would be very grateful if I would not seek his flag as a trophy, and that he would be greatly obliged if I would give it him so that he could show it to his King, holed and torn as it was, as evidence of the valor with which he opposed me. I did not think I ought to refuse to meet his wish, preferring the ingots which I assumed were between decks to the cloth, however glorious it might be. After having thanked me many times, he admitted that he had ladies on board and Monsignor the Apostolic Vicar added that he would be very pleased to see that the filibusters were not as unbelievably cruel and debauched as was everywhere published, and he further said that they were delighted that they had been conquered by the French filibusters rather than the English, because the latter, being heretics, did not show in war the restraint and courtesy usual among subjects of the King of France, who had remained Roman Catholics.

I reassured them, promising on my honor, safe conduct for all, and I assured them that we wanted nothing but the merchandise, and that as regards their persons they would be well treated and would receive their freedom after payment of a ransom, the amount of which I would tell them later. As to the ladies, I gave my word that no harm of any kind would befall them provided they were willing not to show themselves too much to my crew.

Having said this, I had all the weapons surrendered . . . and I busied myself making good, as far as possible, the chaos in the galleon's rigging, assisted by those who remained of the Spanish sailors. All these men were delighted to have saved their skins, both from the storm which terrified them and from the bullets of our guns.

No lady was worried or molested. I must add that of all five of them there was in truth not one who was worth the trouble. And they scarcely showed themselves except to me, who visited them twice or thrice out of courtesy, and they did not leave their rooms where they spent all their time in being tormented by seasickness.

I learned from the galleon's commander that the squall had brought them within an inch of shipwreck . . . Being then quite crippled and drifting from their squadron, they could only let themselves be pushed along by the hurricane. On the morning of the day on which I found them, having no hope of resuming the direction of Spain and crossing the ocean in their present state, they had decided to return towards Cartagena. But we had stopped this voyage. He also told me that we should not have brought his resistance to an end had his soldiers been able to stand on their legs and fight. Not being accustomed to sea voyaging, they never ceased, day or night, to be tormented by their stomachs, from which all food escaped as soon as eaten, so that they were thereby much weakened. . . .

On this galleon were found four hundred and forty large bars of fine Peruvian gold, nine hundred of silver, twelve chests full of pearls from Panama and elsewhere, as well as the rarest and most precious stones, and a quantity of other merchandise and articles of the highest price, of which I will not make an inventory here because it would require volumes.

When the King's part had been put aside, all this brought to us, to myself and all my men, an infinite quantity of goods and abundant wealth and glory besides.

So ends the narrative of Le Golif relating to his capture of the great galleon. It requires a number of comments. In the first place, luck played an important, and possibly a deciding role in the capture of the galleon. Badly crippled in rigging and upper works, the great high-sided vessel could scarcely maneuver except before the wind. Otherwise she could have come about and brought her main batteries to bear on the corsair vessel and virtually blown it out of the water. The seasickness of the armed guard was another crippling factor. No man is a fighting man when overcome with *mal de mer*. Had the weather been calm and the soldiers not ill, they probably could have replied much more vigorously to the small arms fire of the filibusters. Nevertheless, from a purely military point of view, the Spaniards, in spite of their handicaps, put up only feeble resistance.

The merciful treatment accorded to the officers, passengers, crew and soldiers of the galleon was due to Le Golif alone. As a youth he had studied briefly for Holy Orders, and perhaps this accounted for his good treatment of his victims and his gallantry toward the ladies. And we cannot forbear a smile at his blunt remarks about their lack of beauty and appeal!

It should also be borne in mind that Le Golif and the other corsairs or filibusters were *not* pirates, but privateers. The word filibuster is a French derivation of the English word freebooter. France was at war with Spain. Any Frenchman who could arm, equip and man a vessel to prey against the ships of His Catholic Majesty could obtain a letter of marque. Consequently, the rules of warfare rather than the bloody practices of piracy were often followed when a Spanish vessel was captured. On the other hand, ruthless Frenchmen like Montbars the Exterminator and Roc Brasiliano were notorious for their torture of Spanish civilians and mariners and wholesale killings of prisoners.[4]

Privateers and pirates often did not make such an easy capture as described by Le Golif, especially if they were so bold as to attack an armed frigate or man-of-war. Le Golif did so on another occasion and soon had a bloody battle on his hands. After pretending to be mariners whose vessel had been battered by a violent storm, Le Golif and his free-booters approached the frigate in small boats, making believe that they were abandoning their own vessel. Here Le Golif takes up the narrative:

> We drew alongside the ladder and I ascended first, taking care to keep my head lowered and well hidden by my hat like someone overwhelmed by the deepest consternation. But you may well imagine that I went up the last rungs like lightning and, leaving no one the time to recognize me or take it all in, I fired my two pistols almost point blank into the faces of the two officers whom I thought to be of the highest rank. Quicker even than my powder, I next drew my sword and thrust it right and left as much as I could before they had unsheathed their own, and I thereby stretched out half a dozen in less than no time.
>
> My men were now joining me in great clusters, helping themselves up by the [ship's] chains. The enemy was fleeing on all sides, having allowed themselves to be caught without weapons, which they were now running to fetch. Those who had them, having found time to draw, began to face up with

some obstinacy and courage. One of them hurled himself upon me with a great sabre, but I parried his blow and ran him through cleanly, after which I picked up his weapon and held it in my left hand, and was soon well pleased with it, as we shall see.

Having rallied in imposing numbers, they charged us and broke up our company, which I had wanted to hold together. A fine mêlée followed, each man for himself without being able to attend to his neighbor. At one moment I was alone against three of them, two with swords and the last with a sabre. It was then that I saw the fruits of the fine lessons which my good fencing-master . . . had given me. I parried all their blows and thrust all three of them in the belly. I had only just extracted myself when I saw that I had seven on my hands, who assailed me from all sides, armed with pikes, axes and sabres. As soon as I had floored one, two others would run up, so that there were soon more than a dozen pressing in on me. Ridding myself of one of them who had come too close by a great kick in the genitals, and another, who had fallen and sought to stab me from below with his knife, whom I quieted by crushing his face with my heel, it might be well said that I fought with all four limbs, and without any presumption I assert that, so doing, I am, properly speaking, invulnerable and invincible. On that day I even knew how to ward off pistol and musket balls with a twirl of my sabre.

Seeing with whom they were engaged, all these *bougres* began to take care and keep their distance. I charged them at once, which made them flee like a flock of sparrows. There remained only a great devil who raised a huge axe and thought to split my head in two, but before he could do so I nailed him to a rack of belaying pins. I had some difficulty in withdrawing my sword, and was only able to do so by giving him a good push in the belly with my foot. It was then, without doubt, that I received a slight sword thrust in my left shoulder, but I did not become aware of the pain until after the fight. It was given me, I think, by an officer who gave me the greatest trouble in all this merry-making. I fenced with him in a fine fashion, and I was grateful to have two like him before me, since this bully was joined by one of his companions who, by way of greeting, began by firing his two pistols into my face. They only just missed me, for the balls carried away my hat. I was not long in seeing that the man was more expert with a sword than with a firearm, nor in finding myself uncomfortable with these two fellows. But for my courage and steadiness of mind, I would not have come out of it at all. It was then that Pulvérin, my good brother and *matelot* [literally "buddy"] who later became my second in command, saved the situation by coming up behind them with a sabre in his right hand and an axe in his left. He opened the shoulders of one and all the back of the head of the other, and thereby rid me of these heroes who had been two to one.

While we took time to breathe, we saw that our men had rallied together and had already almost mastered the deck between the mainmast and foremast, but that behind the balusters of the forecastle a large number of soldiers, who were lying in wait there under a petty officer full of malice, were preparing to send us a murderous discharge from their muskets. This was no time to hesitate, and it was necessary for us to sweep them all away. I was about to spring forward when they fired. But they were too hasty and their bullets were badly aimed, so that they passed above our ears. We leaped to the attack. At the starboard ladder I was forced to run through several pikemen who aspired to stop me with their weapons, which gave me little to fear; it was enough for me to parry the blow with my sabre and with it to hold the lance low, after which I had plenty of time to pierce the lancer with my sword wherever I liked, and to send him quite nicely to God or the Devil, which I did not fail to do five or six times in succession. Then the others, fearful of such a fate, gave me passage, and I was able to reach the upper deck, where I did great carnage beneath the mizzen.

We were fighting one against ten. Darkness was falling and each had difficulty in recognizing his fellows . . . Several, thinking I was an officer of the King, summoned me to their aid, which was a most desirable convenience to me since, under the guise of helping them, I could slay them without respite. Seeing which, they began to challenge one another and to strike one another with sabre, axe or pike, in the belly and elsewhere, which is by no means usual or courteous between friends. They shouted like demons in order to make themselves known, calling out their names . . . There was less risk for us in this respect, since we had known one another for a long time, while many wore large gold ear rings, which proved for us a very distinctive and recognizable mark. . . . One small youth, doubtless misled by my clothing, cried out on seeing me approach: "Don't kill me, father!"

I had not the least difficulty in showing him, with my sword, that he was mistaken in thinking that I was his father.

It was soon no more than a massacre and for one whose heart was not too hardened it was somewhat distasteful. In the end, those who remained let themselves drop into the lower battery. I have said that we brought grenades with us. We exploded a few of them between their legs. They cried out for mercy, but we sent a few more with the sole object of bringing them completely to wisdom.

However, it was certainly necessary to halt. I had all the hatchways battened down promptly so as to shut the monkeys up, and all of us rejoiced very much at having won an engagement that had begun so badly.

The author of this graphic description was probably exaggerating, especially regarding his own prowess.* Nevertheless it appears to be a reasonably accurate picture of the desperate fighting between attacker and attacked.

Le Golif was one of the few corsairs (or pirates for that matter) who were smart enough to retire from the sea and live out their lives ashore. Most of them kept on roving until they were killed, imprisoned or hanged. During his latter years he occupied himself with writing his memoirs. They

---

* See Appendix, page 209.

remained unknown and undiscovered for more than 250 years. Then, during World War II, following the capture of St. Malo by American forces in August 1944, three bulky manuscript books were found in the cellar of an old house in that town when it was being cleaned up. Part of the pages had fallen into decay in the battered trunk where they had reposed for who knows how long. But enough remained to piece out a remarkable document of the adventures of Le Golif, corsair captain, braggart and lady's man. There is no doubt of the authenticity of the manuscript, for it has been certified as genuine by a number of French authorities and its English publishers.

In recounting the amount of silver, gold and jewels taken from the galleon, it is almost certain that Le Golif was exaggerating. However, precious cargoes such as he describes were not uncommon aboard galleons in those days.

Silver ingots, gold bars and beautifully gem-encrusted jewelry have been recovered from a Spanish wreck off Bermuda in recent years and are on display at the Bermuda Historical Society museum. Silver ingots were stamped with the royal arms, assayers' marks and other means of identifications. The same for gold bars. If Le Golif was telling the truth, his haul could have been worth $10,000,000 in today's purchasing power.

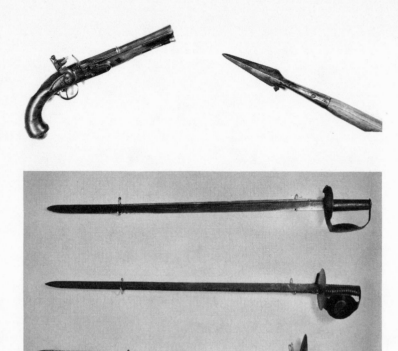

Pirate weapons: (A) (center) Three types of eighteenth-century cutlasses; used in naval warfare. (B) A boarding axe carried in the belt; used
for cutting rigging and smashing doors and hatches—also heads. (C) A
brass-barreled flint-lock pistol. (D) A boarding pike used for offense and
defense aboard ship. (From the author's collection.)

5

Weapons, Women and Wine

T<small>HE</small> muskets used by the pirates were large-caliber weapons, originally intended for hunting wild cattle and hogs on the island of Hispaniola. They were approximately sixty caliber, firing balls weighing an ounce apiece. The bullets were of soft lead and created a large, gaping wound. The pirates were noted for their accuracy in firing their weapons, having acquired great skill as hunters. This probably accounts for their success in attacks on enemy ships and fortifications. Muskets were used mostly for land assaults and for firing on an enemy craft before boarding.[1]

The favorite weapons of the freebooters were pistols, knives, cutlasses, boarding axes and pikes. The flintlock pistols were of large caliber and accurate only at a comparatively short distance. They were fitted with hooks for attaching to the belt or to a broad leather sling across the chest. Only one shot could be fired at a time. There was always the chance of a misfire, due to an incorrectly placed flint or damp priming powder. Therefore a pirate carried several brace of pistols on his person when attacking. The famous pirate Blackbeard who terrified the Atlantic coast during the early part of the eighteenth century was said to have carried twelve pistols.

The cutlass, or sabre as the French corsairs called it, was a short, curved sword that could be used for hacking as well as piercing the body of an opponent. Being short, it did not become entangled in a man's legs. The cutlass had a heavy, single-edged blade sharply tapered for thrusting. The knuckle guard was broad to protect the warrior's hand from being sliced by his opponent. In his belt the attacking pirate carried a short hand ax similar in design to the tomahawk of the American Indians although considerably heavier. It was very useful for chopping rigging, cracking skulls and battering down cabin doors.

Pirates were also adept at the use of hand grenades, or grenados, as they called them. The famous buccaneer Captain Henry Morgan used grenados with great success in storming enemy defenses on the Spanish Main.[2] During an attack at sea, grenados were tossed from one ship to another; and when the pirates boarded their victim they made sure to hurl a few grenados down the hatchways to silence enemy opposition below decks. These grenados were of simple construction, consisting of a hollow iron ball filled with black powder. A tube into which a fuse was inserted contacted the powder. The fuse was cut to a length calculated to explode the grenado at impact point. The iron ball flew into deadly pieces with the explosion.

Another weapon used mostly for defense was the boarding pike. This was similar to a lance, having a pointed iron head fixed to a seven-foot pole. Sometimes for close combat the shafts were shortened to six feet or less. Pikes were very useful in fending off boarders and for hand-to-hand fighting on deck. But unless they were skillfully used, they were of little avail against desperate opponents firing pistols or slashing with ax and cutlass.

No pirate would ever think of going anywhere, day or night, without one or more knives in his belt. These were long for knives; some had single-edged blades, others double-edged. They were similar to poniards or daggers. Sharpened regularly, they were used for such peaceful work as skinning and butchering animals and for cutting meat at mealtime. Pirates found them useful aboard ship and for fighting their enemies or each other.

The ordnance carried aboard pirate ships varied according to the size of the vessel. Some of the small piratical sloops carried as few as four guns of small caliber, shooting a six-, eight- or twelve-pound ball. The larger vessels carried up to forty guns, some of which fired eighteen- or twenty-four-pound shot. These cannon were, of course, muzzle loading and arranged in batteries on either side of the vessel. They could not be aimed except straight ahead or at a very narrow angle, and were fired in broadside fashion. Gunnery in those days was a hit-or-miss affair with many misses. This was due primarily to the fact that the vessel was rarely steady for a moment, tossing and pitching about on the waves. If the cannon was fired when the vessel was on an upswing, the cannon balls often whistled harmlessly over the enemy vessel or through the rigging. If fired on a downswing, the shot plunged into the sea before reaching the target. A favorite maneuver was to sail athwart the enemy's stern or bow and rake the decks with murderous fire. Cannon could be loaded with a variety of deadly missiles. For battering the ship's hull, solid round shot was used. If struck too often below the waterline, the vessel would sink.

For close work in raking the decks, the guns would be loaded with musket balls, or cannister as it was called, which spewed a deadly hail of lead like a giant shotgun. A third missile was chain or bar shot. The chain shot consisted of two balls connected by a length of chain. When fired from a cannon, this chain shot hurtled through the air and sliced through the rigging like a giant knife. The bar shot accomplished the same thing. Both these missiles were used primarily to bring down an enemy's rigging, halting the vessel. If the masts were struck, they often toppled overside, bringing down much of the rigging. Then there was langrage. This consisted of a miscellaneous assortment of nuts, bolts, nails and other pieces of scrap iron useful both for puncturing sails and destroying rigging or killing men about decks.

The cannon were secured by blocks and tackles which not only kept the wheeled carriages in proper position in front of the gun ports but also took up the recoil. After the correct amount of powder had been rammed down the muzzle, wadded, and the shot inserted, a priming charge was placed in the touchhole. This priming charge was powder of a finer grain. The gunner stood at the side of the gun holding a linstock, a forked stick into which a slow-burning match was inserted. The slow match was made of a piece of rope soaked in saltpeter. When ignited, it smoldered slowly. Just before firing, the gunner whirled the linstock about his head to get the slow match glowing. Then at the word "Fire!" he touched it to the priming charge which detonated the cannon.

Splinters were one of the principal causes of casualties aboard armed vessels. When the bulwarks of a vessel were hit by a round shot, large jagged pieces of wood flew in all directions. They acted as great daggers which could transfix a man and kill him as easily as a bullet or a shell fragment.

When approaching an enemy vessel, a number of pirates

would place themselves in the shrouds and foretop as sharp-shooters. From these vantage points they could pick off the officers on the quarterdeck of the opposing vessel.

When a pirate captain decided the time had arrived for boarding, he gave the order "Boarders away!" Stationed along the bulwarks were men equipped with grapnels. These hooks with several prongs were attached to heaving lines, and were hurled across to the other ship and became entangled in the rigging. Then the pirates hauled in the lines and drew the two vessels together. One or more boarding planks were quickly shoved across and the pirates swarmed aboard the enemy.

A pirate vessel would sometimes ram the opposing ship with its bowsprit, entangling the rigging of both vessels and locking them together. This was a dangerous method, because when the time came to disengage, it was often difficult to do so.

Once the opposing ship had surrendered, it was up to the pirate captain to decide what to do with the survivors. The victors were not always as merciful to passengers and crew as was Captain Le Golif after the capture of the Spanish galleon. Usually a pirate commander would offer to spare the lives of all those aboard who were willing to cast their lot with the pirates and go a-roving. Those who refused were often butchered or tossed overboard if there was not enough food to go around. In other instances they were set adrift in small boats to make their way to land as best they could. If the captured ship was badly damaged it would be burned or sunk. If in reasonably good condition it would be made a prize; a prize crew was put aboard and sailed it back to the pirate haven.

Wild celebrations followed the capture of a rich prize. The men rifled the belongings of their victims, dressed themselves in all sorts of elaborate costumes, drank the wine and brandy of the vanquished and sang, yelled, and capered about in great glee. Great gambling games went on with the money taken from the vessel, and it was often difficult for the pirate captain to preserve discipline and keep the ship under weigh.

Some of the more strict pirate captains absolutely forbade gambling aboard their vessels. They even attempted to ration the liquor, although this was not very successful.

The greatest carousing took place ashore upon the arrival of the victorious sea robbers. At their "castle" they would stage a great banquet in honor of their success. Native cooks worked mightily, serving great tureens of sea-turtle soup, boiled beef, and roast pig, with piles of roasted plantains and yams, jellies, sweetmeats, and of course plenty to drink. One of the favorite beverages of the pirates had the mild name of *punch*. It could be made in a variety of ways, but its principal ingredient was rum. If a French ship had been captured, brandy would be substituted. The punch was a strong potion, and guaranteed to put even the most hardened sea rover into a jovial, or sometimes murderous, mood.

Quite often these feasts would end in a free-for-all or a duel between rival pirate captains. One of these is described in a contemporary account. A French corsair captain got into an argument with an Englishman who, the Frenchman claimed, had been disrespectful to his native wife. Here is his story of the affair:

> I could not decently suffer such insults any longer and was not long in drawing my sword.
> "You cursed Calvinistic *bougre*, defend yourself!" I cried. "I am going to make you pay at once for your impudence and make you swallow your own words. . . ."
> "Make room for fair play," shouted the Brethren of the Coast, pushing back the benches and tables.
> I had not reflected that, the better to suit my gentlemanly

costume, I had taken a small dress sword and had left upstairs the good fighting rapier which I usually wear. So that, scarcely had I crossed swords, ... going all out, when I was annoyed to see in no time at all my weapon was bent like a fish hook. I ought to say that droll fellow was quite honest and could have hit me with the greatest ease. Doubtless to swagger before the gallery, he stopped. Pulvérin, my first mate, handed me his skewer which was a Spanish rapier and devilishly good in the hand.

The guests ... formed a large circle with many shouts and jokes, but I was not long in thrusting a foot of steel into the fellow's throat and down he fell, vomiting up his blood in great gushes. His friends stretched him out on a table ... when I saw the men around the table take off their hats and fall suddenly silent I understood that my opponent had just passed away. ... The corpse which was very large and heavy was being removed when a dispute arose and his comrades were quick to fly into a rage. The pirates of both sides went outside and there at once broke out a heated and merry mêlée in which I saw how brave my men were ... The scuffle did not last long and all the accomplices and comrades of the dead man were quickly thrown out. It cost only two scratches from sabres and knives despite the half dozen pistol shots which did not hit anyone and only broke a stoneware plate that was hanging from the wall.

[Returning inside the narrator cried out happily:]

"Gentlemen of the sea and of fortune! Adventurers and warriors of the islands! Mariners of the devil! Put the tables and benches back in their places quickly. Each of you take a seat and open his muzzle and his belly for the Negroes are about to serve us." So we went to the tables with loud cries of real joy and much gaiety. ... The meal was, as I had wished, very abundant and sumptuous. Some ate to excess; there were some who, after the roasts, were powerless to swallow any more; some even had to leave and perform the contrary process outside. ... During the dessert the gaiety developed in a big way.

Most of the quarreling and fights between the pirates was from two causes—gambling and women. One of the most notable duels in the annals of piracy was fought amid a number of beautiful captive women.[3] One of the pirate captains by the name of Captain Fulbert noticed that one of the women was more beautiful and of a nobler bearing than the others. The men were beginning to pinch their bottoms and squeeze their breasts in spite of their cries and resistance. Distressed by the disgust of the noble lady, Captain Fulbert went over to her and cried to the crowd, "I forbid anyone to touch this lady and I take her under my protection!"

The other pirates looked at him, surprised, and began to curse him, reminding him that the Brothers of the Coast had always shared and shared alike. Some of them were drunk. He told them that with women the sharing was different. Women were not to be shared like the rest of the booty. Nevertheless, the pirates kept shouting and demanding that Fulbert give up the woman for their general pleasure.

Their shouts so enraged Fulbert that he drew his sword. There was a great uproar. It looked for a moment as if there would be a mad brawl, for a number of pirates drew their knives. Others half pulled their cutlasses from their scabbards.

At a signal from Fulbert, his crew lined themselves up with him and were ready to fight for their captain. Then Fulbert tore the woman from the clutching hands of his opponents and thrust her into the arms of his best friend, saying, "I know you for an honorable man. I entrust this girl to you while I fight for her, and I swear in Christ's name that none of these shall have her except they disembowel me if they can."

His friend quickly shielded the girl with his own body and then placed her between the table and the wall. He drew his own sword and was ready to support Fulbert in any exchange of steel.

Fulbert meanwhile had leaped to the table and shouted, "You cursed lechers and scurvy whoremongers! I challenge you one after the other, as many as you are, in single combat with any weapon you care to use provided it is of steel, and I shall use my sword!"

It is very probable that Fulbert would have thought twice before issuing such a wholesale challenge, had he been cold sober. But he had drunk enough to make him bold and reckless. His words caused a great commotion among the pirates. They valued courage above everything else and were quite used to duels and hostile encounters between individuals. A duel was something to be watched with great interest, and heavy wagers were made on the outcome.

One of the other captains shouted, "Fair play!" and tables and benches were pushed aside to make a ring in the middle of the room. The pirates grouped themselves around the edges, even forgetting the women for a little while.

Fulbert stood in the center, his sword drawn, waiting for the first volunteer. From out of the crowd came a huge, hulking figure more than six feet tall with great knotted muscles. He had stripped off his shirt and stood there with his hairy chest puffed out and his square chin thrust forward, looking for all the world like a mad bull in the ring at Seville. He had a reputation as a tough fighter with the cutlass, which he used both for cutting and thrusting. Now he drew his weapon, so heavy that he alone had the strength to swing it.

But he was facing the best swordsman in the Americas. Here was a rare opportunity for a man to see which of the two weapons would be really supreme—the sword or the cutlass. Quick bets were placed for one or the other among the murmuring men.

While this was going on, Fulbert's friend was attempting to calm the fright of the beautiful young woman. He assured her that as long as he was her protector she had nothing to fear. She then asked him who this man Fulbert was. He replied that Fulbert was a bold and well-known pirate captain and was considered the finest swordsman of them all.

Now all eyes were on Captain Fulbert who placed himself on guard. The point of his sword pointed straight toward his enemy while his brawny opponent circled around him with the agility of a cat, in spite of his bulk. Suddenly his great cutlass descended in a flashing arc but sliced nothing but thin air. Fulbert had leaped aside, and before the other could raise his weapon, the pirate captain's sword darted between his ribs. The hairy man did not fall. He slashed again with his weapon at the circling Fulbert. Blood was beginning to stream down the hairy chest; his breathing became labored. Suddenly he tottered and fell with an animal grunt, spitting up an ugly froth of blood. Like a bull which had met his fate in the bull ring, the hulking pirate was dragged away and died a few hours later.

The next man to present himself was of smaller stature but very nimble. He too was armed with a cutlass and kept it flashing about in a bright circle. He handled his weapon far better than the other challenger. Several times he struck Fulbert's sword so heavily that it looked as if the blade might snap. The air sang with the clash of steel. Fulbert withstood the onslaught, and when the man with the cutlass attempted to thrust, Fulbert's blade continually forced him backward. So they fought, alternately advancing and retreating, until Fulbert pierced the thigh of his opponent. This did not stop the pirate's impetuous onslaught and for a moment it looked as if he might split Fulbert's head in two. But the agile captain leaped aside and ran his blade through his opponent's shoulder. His cutlass dropped to the ground and he stood there stupidly, his arm dangling, blood flowing from a wound that would leave him crippled forever.

Shouts of derision at the expense of the loser greeted the end of this fight. At least the fellow could console himself that he was still alive.

The third man to present himself caused a murmur of admiration to pass through the crowd. He too had torn off his shirt and strode to the center of the room clutching a heavy battle-ax in each hand. He was a short, squat, heavily built rascal with powerful shoulders and heavy muscles. He advanced on Fulbert like a charging bull. But it was not long before Fulbert put a foot of steel into his guts, quickly withdrawing the blade. Cursing, the axman charged forward and again Fulbert pierced him, this time a little higher, through the chest. The force of Fulbert's forward rush carried him out of the circle and he almost fell. During this scrimmage, the burly pirate brought his axes down with terrific force. Had they struck Fulbert, they would have split him in two from scalp to toes, but they only struck a table, shattering it into splinters. To avoid the blows, Fulbert had leaped to the left, simultaneously thrusting his blade several times through the rib cage of the pirate, who sank to the floor without a sound, his eyes open, arms outstretched.

The fourth challenger made the mistake of being drunk. He had equipped himself with a boarding pike and charged as if he were repelling an onslaught aboard ship. Fulbert parried the thrust, stepped aside and spitted the fellow prettily. As the narrator of this true account wrote later, "He fell, vomiting as much wine as blood."

The fifth man, apparently taking a lesson from the others whom Fulbert had vanquished, now came forward with a cutlass in his right hand and a large butcher's knife in his left. "He was more nimble than a marmoset and a wily fighter." He gave Fulbert much trouble, aiming to tire him, remaining always at a distance and dancing about like a buffoon, so that in the end he was greeted by jeers and scoffed at for cowardice. This so affected his sense of honor that he began to take risks. He tried thrusting. But Fulbert was not long in whipping out one of his eyes in a fine attack to the face. The pirate struck desperately with his knife and succeeded in slashing Fulbert's shoulder. Although half blinded by his wounded eye, the pirate continued to fight for a few minutes more. Then he gave up and threw down his weapons, admitting defeat. Fulbert let him go, whimpering with pain.

The sixth contestant was a puny little fellow who matched himself against Fulbert with a long Spanish rapier. Although the man was a poor physical specimen, he was adroit. He made some fancy passes in the Italian fashion, with low thrusts which Fulbert found difficult to parry. By this time Fulbert was tiring, sweating profusely and losing a good deal of blood which was running down the sleeve of his shirt and along his arm from the shoulder. Nevertheless, with a desperate flurry of thrusts and parries, Fulbert charged his opponent and ran him neatly through the throat.

Remarks the narrator, "Not long before, one would have thought that twenty champions were eager to measure themselves against Fulbert, but those who remained were now less enthusiastic, and, although urged on by their friends, they hesitated to do so. Some went out to fetch sand from the garden and to throw it over the blood which was spreading on the tiles, so that the combatants would run no risk of slipping."

A Portuguese now presented himself in front of Fulbert,

with a number of knives in his belt and one in each hand. Fulbert's friend and second, guessing what the man planned to do, tossed his cloak over to Fulbert. He had just time to roll it around his left arm to protect himself from the first knife the rascal threw from a distance. Fulbert knocked it down in mid-flight with his cloak-covered arm. "There were shouts, some saying that this was treachery, others replying that a knife was as much a steel weapon as a sabre, an axe or a sword; meanwhile the Portuguese was throwing his knives like a savage his arrows. Fulbert could not avoid receiving one of them in the fleshy part of his leg, and another planted itself in the table . . . The others struck the cloak, except the last which went straight to the heart of a brave Brother of the Coast among the spectators . . . He fell dead at once which caused great consternation because he was esteemed by all and was not in the fight."

By this time the Portuguese had thrown all his knives and was now without weapons. He started to turn and flee. Fulbert charged after him, derisively driving his sword into the man's rump, which provoked great laughter.

"Fulbert, who was now limping badly, passed through the middle of the room, which was as long as it was broad, sword in hand, all sweating and bloody and with so wild an air that more than one trembled at the sight."

It might be thought that the fight had now come to an end. But to everyone's surprise an eighth man appeared. He carried a wicked-looking sword like a Turkish scimitar. Apparently he was counting on Fulbert's fatigue. But the captain had recovered his strength sufficiently to attack the man so furiously that he was soon pierced through and through like a pincushion.

Fulbert did not escape unscathed. He received another painful cut on the same shoulder that had already been wounded. Meanwhile the audience had gotten into furious arguments and no one was paying much attention to the last fight because of the uproar. "Some were busy looking after the maimed, three of whom were in a very bad way." Fulbert was exhausted although he was still on his feet awaiting any other adversaries who might show up. His friend, seeing that he was in no state to endure a ninth fight, came to him and told him that he had demonstrated his courage for all to see and that if anyone else questioned it with steel, he, his friend, would take care of him.

At last the uproar subsided. Peace was restored and Fulbert's friend busied himself binding the captain's wounds, for Fulbert could no longer remain on his feet. In a little while the surgeon from Fulbert's ship arrived and dressed the wounds properly and said that he should be conveyed aboard the vessel and remain very quiet.

They placed the wounded man in a chair which was carried by four of his crew and conveyed to a small boat waiting at the dockside.

Fulbert's wounded leg did not heal for a long time. Finally it had to be amputated. According to Le Golif, Fulbert retired from the trade of piracy, married and lived on a West Indian island to a ripe old age.

This massive seventeenth-century iron treasure chest was the type used by wealthy merchants to safeguard their gold and silver, before the advent of paper money. It weighs 200 pounds empty. Handles are extra wide to accommodate two men on each side when carrying. An intricate locking mechanism occupies the entire inside of the lid, covered by a decorative wrought iron shield. This kind of chest was also used by pirates for burying their loot. (From the author's collection.)

6

Colonial Dealers
in Loot

Some of the reasons why such a vast amount of looted East Indian merchandise was shipped to Atlantic seaports by the Red Sea Men are to be found in the economic and political situation that existed in the American colonies during the latter part of the seventeenth century. Like many other European nations at this period, England believed completely in the theory and practice of mercantilism. It was based on the principle that trade could not be mutually advantageous. In every transaction, so the theory went, one party must be the gainer and one the loser. Great Britain wanted to be as nearly self-sufficient as possible. At the same time, the Crown tried to force all its colonies and other countries as well to buy as much as possible from England. The Crown also held that most of the money (gold and silver) should be kept in England. It was British policy that the colonies should be administered like plantations. The Crown encouraged the colonists to produce raw materials needed by the mother country, but through a series of restrictive Navigation Acts the colonies were required to purchase from England most of the manufactured goods they needed. At the same time, Americans were prohibited from developing any raw materials or manufacturing products which would seriously compete with those produced and sold by the mother country.

Bounties were offered to Americans for producing such highly desired raw products as naval stores (turpentine, rosin, tar, etc.), lumber, tobacco, molasses, and whale oil. Yet bounties and preferential duties failed to spur the colonies to increase their production of the favored commodities to any great extent.

Beginning in 1651, a number of acts relating to navigation and trade were passed by the Crown. Their purpose was to exclude foreigners, primarily the rival Dutch, from commerce with British colonies. These laws provided further assurance that England should be the focus of the commercial activities of the colonies and that "British workmen should not lack raw materials nor the manufacturers a colonial market for their wares."

As a result, American colonials were forced to buy all their merchandise from England, often at high prices and as often of poor quality. The prosperous merchants and planters, hungry for luxury items, were prohibited from buying them from the French, Spanish, or Dutch. Many products exported by these nations were highly desired, including wine, olive oil, spices, raisins, many types of cloth, ivory, shoes, and jewelry.

Inevitably, smuggling became a thriving business all along the Atlantic coast. This was particularly true from Massachusetts Bay Colony south to the Carolinas, for the Atlantic coast line with its many inlets, bays, and rivers made smuggling easy and profitable.

To be a smuggler required a certain measure of shrewdness, seafaring knowledge and courage. It was not a long leap from smuggling to privateering, and, when opportunity offered, from privateering to piracy.

Such was the situation during the last half of the seventeenth century. When the first shipload of loot from the Red Sea area was smuggled into the port of New York, the exotic merchandise was quickly snapped up by local merchants at a fraction of its original cost. No one asked where the stuff came from, although everyone knew. Over a generous number of glasses of rum, it was whispered that there was much more merchandise to be had from the Malabar Coast and Red Sea ports. These dealings worked both ways. Colonial merchants were only too eager to supply "honest mariners" or privateers with provisions, gear and armaments in return for cargoes of fine silks, cloth of gold, ivory, perfumes and precious gems. Thus started active and open transactions between the Red Sea Men and the merchants of Boston, New York, Providence, Newport, Philadelphia and other ports.

It was early in 1684 that the trade grew to a sufficiently large volume to be noted by Governor Cranfield of New Hampshire. At this time he wrote to the Lords of Trade in London expressing worry over the whole business. He described the arrival of a pirate vessel in Boston with booty he estimated to be worth £700 per man. So eager for the cargo were the merchants of Boston that they sent out their own pilot to bring the ship safely to anchor.

During the next twenty-five years merchants of the Atlantic coast and the West Indies grew fat and wealthy on pirate loot. At the same time some of the more unctuous publicly declared their horror and antipathy to the practice of piracy, decrying it as a social evil and "a cancer on the body politic." But just as today, when a prominent industrialist has a public relations specialist at his elbow, so in the olden time merchants, politicians and churchmen had a knack of presenting a pious face to the public while they worked in secret as fences for high seas robbers.

The big boom in pirate trade began almost immediately after the arrival of Colonel Benjamin Fletcher, who became the Governor of New York in 1694. His character is well described in a letter dated June 13, 1695, from Peter De La Noy to a friend in London:

I remember the remark you made when our present Govern'r was sent hither, viz. That he was a necessitous man who you feared would therefore consider the advancement of his own private fortunes rather than the publick benefit of the Province; and I can now assure you we found you a true prophet, and wish you could foretell our deliverance as well as you did our oppression from this arbitrary man.

At his first arrival here he insinuated with the inhabitants the great interest and credit he had at Whitehall, which would baffle any complaints that could be made against his administration and this back'd with the grandeur of his Coach and six horses (a pomp this place had never seen in any former Govern'r no more than himself been us'd to it in his own country) struck such a terror into the people as easily prepared 'em for the pack-saddles he has laid upon 'em. To recount all his acts of squeezing money both out of the publick and private purses would make a volume instead of letters . . .

He takes a particular delight in having presents made to him, declaring he looks upon 'em as marks of their esteem of him, and he keeps a catalogue of the persons who show such good manners, as men most worthy of his favour. This knack has found employment for our silversmiths and furnished his Excellency with more plate (besides a variety of other things), than all our former Governors ever received.

Although nearly three hundred years have passed since that letter was written, it remains rich in human emotion, cynicism and an occasional flash of humor. It is the same with many of the other documents of this period which were studied by the author in the preparation of this book. American colonials and English officials of the eighteenth century were adept at writing letters and reports that eloquently expressed their thoughts and feelings.

De La Noy's letter continued:

We have a parcell of pirates in these parts which [people] call the Red Sea Men, who often get great bootys of Arabian Gold. His Excellency gives all due encouragement to these men, because they made all due acknowledgement to him; one Coats, a captain of this "honorable order," presented his Excellency with his ship, which his Excellency sold for £800 and every one of the crew made him a suitable present of Arabian gold for his protection; one Captain Twoo [Tew] who is gone to the Red Sea upon the same errand was before his departure highly caressed by his Excellency in his coach and six horses and presented with a gold watch and engaged him to make New York his port on his return. Twoo retaliated the kindness with a present of jewells; but I can't learn how much farther the bargain proceeded; time must shew that.

Fletcher's hobnobbing with known pirates was an open scandal in New York and throughout the colonies. In 1698 when Fletcher was recalled to London in disgrace, he wrote answers to all charges in a vain effort to clear himself. Here is what he said about his association with the pirate Tew:

As for my intimacy and kindness with Captain Tew and the great presents from him which is objected, this is the truth and the whole truth of that poore affair.

This Tew appeared to me to be not only a man of courage

and activity, but of the greatest sence and rememberance of what he had seen, of any seaman I had mett. He was allso what they call a very pleasant man; soe that at some times when the labours of my day were over it was some divertisement as well as information to me, to heare him talke. I wished in my mind to make him a sober man, and in particular to reclaime him from a vile habit of swearing. I gave him a booke to that purpose; and to gaine more upon him, I gave him a gunn of some value. In return hereof he made me also a present which was a curiosity and in value not much; and this is the sum of all my kindness I am charged with; for as to the coming sometimes to my table, which I think was such as becomes my character, and hospitable to all, I hope that will not stick upon me, if your Lordships but inquire what others have done and still continue to doe in that kind.

Thus did the hypocritical and lying Colonel Fletcher describe the manner in which he "caressed" the pirate Tew. But Thomas Weaver, Agent for the Province of New York, gives us an entirely different picture:

Colonel Fletcher saith likewise that he gave them [Captains Tew, Hoare and others] commissions as privateers for their bravery and courage, which are truest qualifications for great mischief in these men, who were known to be of no moralls, but of the most dissolute principles as well as lewd and infamous behaviour. And it is generally reported by the inhabitants of New Yorke, that to Colonel Fletcher's own knowledge and in his own company they violated the laws of God and man by drunkeness, blasphemy and swearing. Tew was known to Coll. Fletcher to have been a pyrate before (which is seldome without the stain of murder) and yet Colonel Fletcher intrusts him with another commission on the credit of his pious oaths never to practice it again. Hoare was much given to drunkeness and swearing, yet . . . commanded Colonel Fletcher's cellar and servants and committed excesses of debauchery in the Government house and company. Yet these scums . . . are entertained by Colonel Fletcher with the warmest caresses, high drinking and commissions. And it is naturall to believe that these favours were bestowed for better reasons then Tew's being a pleasant man and Colonel Fletcher's wishing to make him a sober man by a present of a book (which it may well be presumed he never made use of) and a gunn, which it is believed he made use of in pyracy.

Now let us return to the time of Fletcher's administration and take notice of some more of his rascally actions. Like some politicians of today, Fletcher surrounded himself with men of substance, the cream of the mercantile trade, who moved in the highest levels of New York society. Among them were Frederick Philipse, the Van Cortlandts, the Van Rensselaers, Godfrey Dellius, the Heathcoates, Nicholas Bayard, William Pinhorne, William Nicoll and William "Tangier" Smith. This group was a nice little, tight little organization of friends and business associates. Many of them were related by marriage. So what could be more convenient to a new and unscrupulous governor than to have these gentlemen as members of his Council? Since he knew he must control judicial matters where traffic with pirates was concerned, Fletcher and his friends secured a monopoly of judgeships of the superior courts and even controlled lower judicial offices and the military.

Not only did Governor Fletcher appoint his cronies to these important offices, but he also granted them vast tracts of land along the Hudson River. This enabled the New York merchants to establish baronial estates and employ many tenant farmers. They formed themselves into a landed aristocracy which rivaled the wealthy planters of Virginia.

Everything fitted very nicely and profitably together. Although Fletcher's political opponents and other honest folk openly charged him with profiting from piracy, he shrugged off the whole matter. Since he controlled the judiciary, the constables and other minor officials, he did not worry.

Another little trick which Fletcher used to aid the pirates was to require bonds guaranteeing that they were setting out upon legitimate trading or privateering voyages. They gave these bonds willingly, for they knew they were fraudulent, and the governor's secretary was in on the whole deal.

Later, in answer to the accusation that he issued privateering commissions to known pirates such as Thomas Tew, Fletcher retorted, "Surely you could not expect me to have known that at the time I issued a Letter of Marque to Captain Tew that he intended to commit acts of piracy on the high seas. You must remember, sir, that once a vessel leaves this port I have no jurisdiction over it whatever. If the captain chooses to abandon legitimate enterprises and turn pirate, there is nothing I can do about it.

"I have never," he maintained, "knowingly given protection to pirates, nor have I dealt with them in any way whatsoever."

Fletcher's loud denials fitted badly with his actions. When Thomas Tew arrived back in New York after a most successful pirate expedition to the Red Sea, he was again welcomed cordially by Governor Fletcher, entertained in his mansion and dined at his table. The two cronies were observed eating and drinking together and conversing over their wine far into the night. Tew was also seen sitting next to the Governor in his carriage. This, said the good citizens, was an outrage, since the Governor's carriage was paid for at the expense of the colony.

Many of the great fortunes of colonial days were based on two main sources of wealth: land grants and traffic with pirates. This was particularly true in the Province of New

York, for Governors Andros and Fletcher were scandalous in robbing the Indians of their lands along the Hudson and giving these tracts to officials and merchants who could be useful to them. A number of these merchants married wealthy women and thus added to their fortunes. For example:

Stephen DeLancey was a refugee from France after the revocation of the Edict of Nantes. He came to New York in 1686 and married Anne Van Cortlandt. A contemporary says of him: "By virtue of his success in business, his marriage into the Van Cortlandt family and the rigorous part he took in politics of the city and province, he had a prominent place in the provincial aristocracy." But what the record did not state was that most of his fortune came from acting as a fence for the sale of stolen merchandise supplied him by the pirates.

Stephanus Van Cortlandt was another prominent merchant of the day. He was the son of Oloff Van Cortlandt, who arrived in New Amsterdam in 1638, became a storekeeper, a real estate operator and city treasurer from 1657 to 1664. He also served long terms as burgomaster.

Stephanus quickly became proficient in community affairs. His business and political interests were not seriously interrupted by the English seizure of New Amsterdam, for Stephanus soon found favor with the new regime.

He married well. His spouse was Gertrude, daughter of Philip Schuyler of Albany. He worked hand in glove with dishonest English officials and connived with them to import goods contrary to the English Acts of Trade. It was not a very great step from smuggling to outfitting Red Sea Men for piratical cruises against the ships of the Great Mogul and the English East India Company.

In 1698 when he was appointed Commissioner of Customs and Inspector of Revenues by Governor Fletcher, he sat back and did nothing. When Lord Bellomont became the Governor, he wrote in 1700 to the Lords of Trade that Van Cortlandt "gives a just account of all the money that comes to his hands, but he is grown very crazy and infirm, and is a very timorous man. In a word he has never yet made any seizure since his being Collector and I believe never would if he were fifty years to come in the post."

Lord Bellomont's estimate of Van Cortlandt's ability to collect legal customs duties is most accurate. Since he was virtually a partner of certain pirates and a smuggler as well, it is not surprising that the royal revenues suffered.

Among the New York merchants of this period no one was more wealthy or influential than Frederick Philipse. In 1647, when he was twenty-one years old, he accompanied Peter Stuyvesant to New Amsterdam. His trade was that of a carpenter. But upon arrival in the New World he quickly branched out into mercantile trade. Apparently he was so busy working that he had few thoughts of marriage until the age of thirty-six when he was wed to Margaret Hardenbrook, a wealthy widow whose husband, Peter De Vries, had been an important shipowner. With the backing of his wife's money and vessels, the enterprising Frederick developed a lucrative trade between New York and the West Indies. Later he expanded this to the East Indies. His first wife died in 1662. She had served Frederick's purposes excellently with her money. Upon her death he married Catherine Van Cortlandt, widow of John Dervall. Dervall also had been in the shipping business and amassed a modest fortune. Thus Frederick Philipse through two marriages and his own enterprise became the wealthiest man in New York. Possessing a comfortable fortune, his mind turned to politics and he was soon on intimate terms with Governor Fletcher. Not long after, Fletcher appointed him to the Council, where he served until 1698. Thanks also to Governor Fletcher, Philipse received extensive grants of land in the county of Westchester bordering the Hudson River. These various parcels he welded into a baronial estate which he called Philipsburg, now known as Philipse Manor. His mansion was called Castle Philipse, a rambling structure typical of Dutch colonial architecture. Fortunately it has been preserved and is now open to the public.

Historians generally agree that Frederick Philipse was the chief intermediary between the Red Sea Men and colonial merchants. He kept five ships plying regularly between New York and Madagascar. It is hardly surprising that his great iron chests should be brimming with Arabian gold, silver pieces of eight and great Spanish doubloons.

Here is a typical example of one method he used to evade the law: Expecting the arrival of one of his ships from Madagascar he sent his sloop *Frederick*, in command of his son Adolphus, to meet her secretly. The *Frederick* had cleared New York, falsely claiming she was bound for a Virginia port. After cruising for some time near the agreed-upon rendezvous, the two vessels met. The one from Madagascar immediately began transferring a large quantity of East Indian goods, including valuable muslins, to the *Frederick*. Then wily Adolphus brought the Madagascar ship boldly into New York with nothing aboard but a number of African slaves which, at that time, were legitimate imports. The sloop, meanwhile, lay secretly in Delaware Bay and discharged her precious and illicit cargo. Then she proceeded to Hamburg. Somehow the British Resident there got wind of the irregular affair, seized the vessel and sent her crew to London for trial. The captain, Perkings, was blamed by Frederick Philipse for the whole affair. Apparently the Lords of Trade in London accepted Philipse's alibi, for it is recorded that they gave Philipse a gentle slap on the wrist by observing, "It does not look well for Philipse to imploy a man of such character."

Philipse's right-hand man was Samuel Burgess. Burgess was what would be known today as a traveling sales executive. In those days he was called a roving factor. He was born in New York and was quite well educated for that day. As a sturdy teen-ager he wangled a letter of marque and went privateering in the Caribbean. Cotton Mather, the strait-laced Protestant clergyman of Boston, thundered invectives against privateering. It was, he said, a breeding ground of piracy. And so it surely was. A letter of marque issued by a responsible government official always put a time limit on the privateering expedition. But many privateers paid no attention to such time limits and went merrily on their way, plundering shipping even after peace between England and her enemies had been declared. This was the case with Sam Burgess as it had been with his famous predecessor, Captain Henry Morgan, who sacked the rich city of Panama after peace had been established between England and Spain. News traveled slowly in those days and the excuse always was that the commander had not received any notice of the cessation of hostilities. It was well known in New York that Burgess was robbing on the high seas, but it was shrugged off as a matter of little concern.

Soon after his return to New York he signed on as mate of a vessel belonging to Frederick Philipse and bound for Madagascar. Here they loaded a valuable cargo and returned to New York. They ran the ship aground at Sandy Hook, removed the cargo, smuggled it in, and scuttled the vessel. Like the three oriental monkeys, government officials heard no evil, saw no evil and spoke no evil!

Sam Burgess was a combination trader, pirate and salesman, an ideal roving representative for crafty Frederick

Philipse. We know a good deal about his life. Unlike Captain Avery, Sam Burgess was as clever in furthering his own interests ashore as he was at sea. He married a niece of Frederick Philipse and not only became a member of the powerful family, but also part of that tight little inner circle of merchants who were rapidly expanding their trade with the Red Sea Men.

Not long after Burgess's marriage, Philipse found that the dividends from the Red Sea voyages were so great that another ship should be built. This was designed especially for pirate trade. Her commander was none other than young, adventurous Sam Burgess. His first voyage was very successful, for Philipse cleared £5000 after all expenses. This amount was derived from the sale of Negro slaves, high passenger fares from Red Sea Men returning home, and the sale of looted merchandise from the Far East.

Burgess continued to impress Philipse with his sagacity to such an extent that the great merchant allowed Burgess to select the kind of cargo for the eastward voyage that was best calculated to reap the greatest profits. Knowing the habits and preferences of his pirate pals, Burgess crammed his vessel with hogsheads of wine and beer. When he arrived at Manaret on the west coast of Madagascar, he was greeted with loud huzzas and the joyful firing of cannon by the pirates; and when the news spread that the vessel was filled with wine and beer, the whole city cheered. He sold the cargo at his own price and replaced the empty holds with pirate loot and "black ivory," as Negro slaves were then euphemistically called. This time Burgess's voyage netted Frederick Philipse £10,000, and of course Sam received his cut.

There seemed to be no end to Sam Burgess's success. His third voyage netted £20,000. Following a short rest ashore, he once more set out for the Red Sea. His old acquaintances at Madagascar again welcomed him and poured gold and silver into his lap for the cargoes he brought them.

The homeward-bound voyage was uneventful until the vessel reached the Cape of Good Hope. Anchored there was the frigate *Loyal Merchant*, commanded by Captain Lowth of the Royal Navy. Before Burgess could clear for action, Lowth had his guns aimed at him and seized the whole ship's company. They were promptly transported to Madras in India and taken before the Governor. Burgess's pirate passengers were quite unconcerned by this turn of affairs. They thought themselves fully protected by His Majesty's Act of Grace which they had accepted before leaving St. Mary. But the Governor of Madras paid no attention to their claims of immunity under the King's Pardon. Everyone was thrown into jail except a handful of veteran sea rovers who had had previous experience with the fluid character of the King's Pardon. They managed to escape with part of their gold aboard an outward-bound vessel.

Burgess was captured in August 1699. Although he might have expected to be sprung by his patron and relative, Frederick Philipse, he languished in prison for a whole year. He arrived in England in August of 1700 and was confined in the Marshalsea Prison in London until his trial. It did not take long for a conviction of piracy to be handed down and it looked very much as if Sam Burgess would end his career with a hempen collar around his neck.

Among other pirates awaiting trial in London was Robert Culliford, a good friend of Burgess, for the two men had gone pirating many a time in the Red Sea. To save his own neck Culliford testified against Burgess. His testimony was welcomed by the Lords of the Admiralty because they were determined that Burgess should hang. It seemed as if it was only a matter of days before this pirate would be jerked into the devil's arms. Then a serious hitch occurred. The solicitor for the Admiralty, being a stickler for English law, found out that it would not be possible for Culliford to testify legally until the Admiralty received written evidence that he had actually received the King's Pardon. He, too, like Burgess's pirate passengers, had submitted to the Act of Grace. After days of waiting and, no doubt, great anxiety on Culliford's part, the document finally arrived, proving that Culliford had actually submitted to the Act of Grace. Consequently Culliford was let out of jail and at the same time Samuel Burgess received his document which was a sentence of death.

During the year or more between Burgess's capture and his sentence of death, his patron Frederick Philipse had not been idle. He had pulled all strings possible in London to save his relative but got nowhere. The record is not clear just whose influence was brought into play. But to everyone's surprise, the Bishops of London and Canterbury were successful in obtaining Burgess's pardon. No one was more surprised than Burgess and no one more chagrined than the Lords of the Admiralty.

One might expect that having escaped the noose by a hair's breadth, Burgess would return to New York and devote his time to law-abiding pursuits. Not he. He was so enamored of the life of a sea rover that he shipped as mate on a privateer and made a voyage to the South Seas. Returning to London, he remained ashore for a whole year. It is not known whether he was ill or tried to reform or both. In any case he returned to Madagascar, took part in capturing a large vessel from the pirate owners, had his house burned down, and took part in local cattle wars. After five years of catch-as-catch-can existence, Burgess was poisoned during a drinking bout by one of the local kings of Madagascar. Thus ended the life of a man who could have become a respectable merchant had he chosen a more prosaic but legal life.

Hand-to-hand fighting between pirates and the crew of the East Indiaman Triton. Axes, pikes, pistols, cutlasses and knives are shown in fierce action. In a melée such as this, it was every man for himself. (From an old print.)

7

Libertatia,
Pirate Republic

ALTHOUGH the vast majority of pirates were cruel, ignorant and bloodthirsty men, there were a few exceptions. For
example, Captain Henry Morgan was accused of inhuman
treatment toward his Spanish prisoners, torturing them to
discover where they had hidden their gems, gold and silver.
This has been disproved, as evidenced by the fact that
shortly after John Esquemeling published *The Buccaneers
of America* in 1684, Morgan sued him for libel and won his
case. A number of French corsairs were highly educated
gentlemen. One or two were noblemen.

The most remarkable trio of pirates among the Red Sea
Men consisted of Captain Misson, Captain Caraccioli and
Captain Thomas Tew. Each of them was a character in his
own right, an individualist, courageous and intelligent. Together, they founded a pirate republic, propounded ad-

vanced ideas on the abolition of slavery, and prohibited the death penalty for crime.

Captain Misson appears first on the piratical stage. Misson, whose first name we do not know, was born in Provence in France of an ancient and honorable family. His father was wealthy. Having a great number of brothers and sisters, young Misson felt that his future depended largely on himself and the kind of fortune he could carve out with his sword. He had received a good education for those days and attended the famous University of Angers, where he studied humanity, logic and mathematics. When he returned home from the university his father offered to secure him a commission in the famous French Musketeers. But young Misson had a different idea. He had read books of travel and adventure and was enthralled with the carefree, roving life of a privateer. So he told his father that he wished to follow the sea, which, he said, "abounds with more variety and would afford me an opportunity to gratify my curiosity by the change of countries."

His father, agreeing to his son's objective, obtained a berth for him aboard the *Victoire*, a French man-o'-war commanded by M. Fourbin, a relative of young Misson's family.

The ship was moored at Marseilles and soon after Misson came aboard, it set off on a cruise in the Mediterranean. He quickly fell in love with the life of a seaman.

"I was resolved to be a complete sailor," Misson wrote. "I was always one of the first on a yardarm, either to hand or reef and very inquisitive on the different methods of working a ship. My discourse was turned on no other subject, and I would get the boatswain and carpenter to teach me in their cabins the constituent parts of a ship's hull and how to rig her which I generously paid 'em for."

While the ship was at Naples, young Misson received

leave to go to Rome, which he had always had a great desire to visit. Having been brought up as a devout Catholic, he was shocked to observe the licentious lives led by the clergy at that time (about 1690) and their luxurious surroundings. In his memoirs he noted sadly, "I began to figure to myself that all religion was no more than a curb upon the minds of the weaker, which the wiser sort yielded to in appearance only." At this psychological moment Misson became acquainted with a young priest to whom he had made his confession. This priest amazed Misson with his advanced and revolutionary ideas about religion.

After the two became friends, the priest did not hesitate to unburden himself to Misson. The life of a religious, he declared, was very good where a man had a subtle, enterprising genius and some friends. A smooth tongue and influence were absolutely necessary to rise to eminence in the hierarchy of the Church, he maintained. He pointed out that the ecclesiastical state was governed with the same policy as were secular principalities and kingdoms. "What is beneficial, not what is meritorious and virtuous, is alone regarded." The young priest's name was Signor Caraccioli.

"There are no more hopes for a man of piety and learning in the patrimony of St. Peter, than in any other monarchy, nay rather less," declared Caraccioli. "For my part I am quite tired of the farce and will lay hold on the first opportunity to throw off this masquerading habit for, by reason of my age, I must act an under part many years; and before I can rise to share the spoils of the people, I shall, I fear, be too old to enjoy the sweets of luxury. I am apprehensive I shall never act up to my character and carry through the hypocrite with art enough to rise to any considerable post in the Church. My parents did not consult my genius or they would have given me a sword, instead of a pair of beads."

Young Misson was so impressed with the logic of Caraccioli, his intelligence and education, that he suggested that he volunteer for service aboard the *Victoire*. Caraccioli leaped at the proposal and promptly cast off his priestly habit. Thanks to the recommendation of his friend, the ex-priest was enlisted aboard the French man-o'-war.

The *Victoire* was a frigate pierced for forty guns but mounting only thirty. Not long after she set sail for Leghorn, she engaged two Algerian pirate vessels and a bloody battle took place. When the captain gave the word to board the corsair vessel, Misson and Caraccioli were the first to leap to obey. The attempt to board the pirates was unsuccessful and Caraccioli was wounded in the thigh. But at the second try the French seamen carried the deck and slaughtered the Algerians. As Misson was fighting, he noticed that one of the Algerians jumped down the main hatch with a lighted slow match. Suspecting his purpose, Misson plunged after him and cut him down just as he was about to set fire to the powder magazine.

Following the defeat of the Algerians, the *Victoire* engaged a number of enemy vessels, including the English *Mayflower*, a merchant ship of eighteen guns. It is noteworthy that French privateers and even French pirates treated their prisoners with greater mercy and gallantry than any other nation. When Captain Balladine of the *Mayflower* was received on board the *Victoire*, he was treated with great civility and was told that neither he nor his men would be stripped. It was a common practice among seafaring conquerors at this period to strip the vanquished officers and men of their clothing and valuables, leaving them only a pair of breeches. On this occasion, the captain declared, "None but cowards ought to be treated after that manner; brave men ought to treat such, though their enemies, as brothers; a gallant man who does his duty ill, speaks a revenge which cannot proceed but from a coward's soul."

Misson and Caraccioli engaged in a number of other battles while aboard the man-o'-war, yet did not find that their fortunes had improved. Soon an opportunity presented itself, however, of which they were quick to take advantage.

The *Victoire* was cruising in the Caribbean and while off the island of Martinique met with the *Winchelsea*, an English man-o'-war of forty guns, commanded by a Captain Jones. Neither vessel hesitated to attack the other and a very smart engagement followed. What happened next is told in Misson's memoirs: "The first broadside killed the captain, the second captain and the three lieutenants on board the *Victoire* and left only the master who would have struck." (That is, lowered his colors and surrendered.)

Misson wrote that, not dismayed, he

took up the sword, ordered Caraccioli to act as a lieutenant and encouraging the men, fought the ship six glasses[1] when by some accident the *Winchelsea* blew up and not a man was saved but Lieutenant Franklin whom the French boats took up and he died in two days . . . After this engagement Caraccioli came to Misson and saluted him Captain, and wished to know whether he would choose a momentary or lasting command; that he must now determine, for at his return to Martinique it would be too late and he might depend upon the ship he fought and saved being given to another, and they would think him well rewarded if made a lieutenant, which piece of justice he doubted: that he had his fortune in his hands which he might either keep or let go; if he made the choice of the latter, he must never again expect she would court him to accept her favors. That he ought to set before his eyes his circumstances, as a young brother of a good family with nothing to support his character; and the many years he must serve at the expense of his blood before he could make any figure in the world; and consider the wide difference between the commanding and being commanded; that he might with the ship he had underfoot and the brave fellows under his command, bid defiance to the power of Europe, enjoy everything he wished, reign sovereign of the southern seas, and lawfully make war on all the world, since it would deprive him of that liberty to which he had a right by the laws of nature.

From the record it is plain that this Caraccioli was a man of great persuasive powers and not lacking in oratorical ability. He argued so sensibly that young Misson decided to follow his advice. He called all hands to the quarterdeck and told them that he had been elected their chief and would devote himself to a life of liberty. He did not intend to force any man or be guilty of injustice; if there were any who did not want to follow his fortune in which he promised to share equally with all, they could step forward and he would set them ashore and they could make their way home.

"They one and all cried, '*Vive le Capitain Misson et son Lieutenant le Scavant Caraccioli.*'" After thanking them for the honor they had conferred on him, Misson promised he would use the power they gave him for the public good and hoped, as they had the bravery to assert their liberty, that they would be unanimous in preserving it and stand by him as they promised to do. Caraccioli became second in command as lieutenant and a schoolteacher was chosen as second lieutenant.

Then a discussion arose as to what flag they should fly. The boatswain, who evidently was an old pirate, said that the black flag was the most terrifying. Caraccioli said no. They were no pirates, but men who resolved to assert that liberty which God and nature gave them. They should have a white ensign with "Liberty" painted on it and the motto "*A Deo a Libertate*"—For God and Liberty—as an emblem of their uprightness and resolution.

For a pirate (which he was, despite his high-sounding

words), Captain Misson was a remarkable fellow. He had a highly developed sense of justice and mercy, was an ardent advocate of liberty and the equality of man under God. Lieutenant Caraccioli was likewise dedicated to the freedom of the individual and independence of thought in every area, including religion.

After shouting, "Liberty! We are free men!", Misson addressed his crew:

> Since you have unanimously resolved to seize upon and defend your liberty which ambitious men had usurped, I recommend that you display a brotherly love to each other; the banishment of all private piques and grudges and a strict agreement and harmony among yourselves. In throwing off the yoke of tyranny I hope that none of you will follow the example of the tyrants, and turn your back upon justice; for when equity is trodden underfoot, misery, confusion and mutual distress naturally follow.

Then he added a warning; he said that his crew would probably be branded with the invidious name of *pirates;* that their enemies would consider themselves meritorious in destroying them.

> Self-preservation therefore, and not a cruel disposition obliges me to declare war against all such as should refuse our entry into their ports, and against all who should not immediately surrender and give up what their necessities require; but in a more particular manner against all European ships and vessels, which are our implacable enemies. And I do now declare such a war, and, at the same time, recommend to you my comrades, a humane and generous behavior toward your prisoners which will appear by so much more the effects of a noble soul, as we are satisfied we should not meet the same treatment should our ill-fortune, or more properly our disunion, or want of courage, give us up to their mercy.

Having delivered himself of this address, Misson ordered the vessel to set sail.

They cruised the Caribbean for several months, capturing a number of ships containing valuable merchandise. The prisoners were treated well. Some joined Misson and his crew. He now determined to dispose of the captured merchandise at the best price. To do this, he took the name of Fourbin, the deceased captain of the *Victoire*. He wrote to the governor of Cartagena, bribed him with rich presents, and succeeded in selling him the captured merchandise at bargain prices. The prisoners were landed and the governor was so pleased with the deal that he sent Misson's ship a quantity of fresh provisions.

All this time, the *Victoire* passed for what she actually had been—a French man-o'-war. She did not arouse any suspicions, except on the part of the British who had several frigates in the vicinity. But Misson was able to elude them.

After cleaning the ship's bottom in a secluded bay on the north side of Cuba, a council of war was held to decide what course they should now steer. Some were for stretching over to the African coast while others declared for New England. Misson himself was for going to the coast of Guinea where they might reasonably expect to meet with valuable prizes. There was also a chance of running athwart East Indian ships, usually loaded with money and merchandise for the East Indian trade. Misson's logic convinced the crew and they set sail.

One of the captures made on the Guinea coast was the *Nieuwstadt* of Amsterdam. Aboard was gold dust to the value of about £2000 and seventeen slaves.

Misson's attitude toward these poor black men is remarkable, considering the period in which he lived. He ordered them to be clothed out of captured stores. He also declared,

The trading for men of our own species can never be agreeable to the eyes of divine justice. No man has the power of the liberty of another, and while those who profess a more enlightened knowledge of the Deity sold men like beasts, they proved that their religion was no more than grimace and that they differed from the barbarians in name only, since their practice was in nothing more humane. For my part, I hope I speak the sentiments of all my brave companions. I have not exempted my own men from the galling yoke of slavery and asserted my own liberty, to enslave others. Although these men are distinguished from Europeans by their color, customs or religious rites, they are the work of the same Omnipotent Being and imbued with equal reason. Wherefore I desire that they be treated like free men—for I would banish even the name of slavery from among them.

He then divided the slaves into two groups, mixing them with the white men so that they could learn the French language and become useful seamen.

It is indeed noteworthy that such antislavery sentiments, including the idea of equality, were voiced by a humane pirate more than 150 years before Lincoln declared that all men were created free and equal. It need hardly be added that the slaves were joyful at their deliverance and became competent mariners.

A number of other ships were captured on the west coast of Africa, after which the *Victoire* proceeded to the Cape of Good Hope and anchored about ten leagues to the northward of Table Bay. No sooner had they cast anchor than they met with an English ship of forty guns which Misson promptly boarded. He found a quantity of English broadcloth and about £60,000 in English crown pieces and Spanish pieces of eight. The English captain was killed in the fight. Captain Misson gave him full honors of war and he was buried on shore. Then Misson ordered one of his men, who had been a stonecutter before turning to the more lucrative trade of piracy, to erect a headstone with the following inscription: *"Ici gist un brive anglais."* (Here lies a gallant Englishman.)

Captain Misson kept the English vessel as a prize and appointed Caraccioli captain. So charmed were the English seamen with Misson's humanity that thirty of them joined his crew and that of Caraccioli. He now had two ships well manned with resolute fellows. After doubling the Cape of Good Hope they reached the south end of Madagascar. During this voyage one of the Englishmen told Captain Misson about the island of Johanna. This place, he said, contained a port where European ships bound for Surat replenished their water and provisions. It would be a good place, he added, to use as a base for forays on English East India Company ships and those of the Great Mogul.

The island of Johanna was ruled by a woman who held the title of Queen Regent, together with her brother. Their deadly enemies were the inhabitants of a neighboring island called Mohilla.

Misson and his pirates were well received by the Queen, who entertained them with feasting and hunting. In the midst of this revelry the King of Mohilla made a raid on Johanna and alarmed the entire populace.

The Queen and her brother persuaded Misson and his men to wage war on Mohilla. From then on a series of attacks and counterattacks took place between the natives of the two islands. Thanks to Misson's men and their vessels and the weight of metal from their cannon, they routed the Mohillans, who quickly sued for peace.

Tiring of this internecine war, Misson was anxious to go back to cruising. He did so and soon captured a large Portuguese ship of sixty guns. The fight lasted from dawn until

two in the afternoon. When the Portuguese captain fell
with a bullet in his brain, the vessel struck her colors and the
pirates boarded and made good their prize. Down below
they found gold dust to the value of £250,000, which today
would be worth approximately ten million dollars. One
unique feature of this fight was that the native wives of Misson, Caraccioli and the other officers were on board and refused to go below during the heavy engagement. Misson
recorded: "The women never quitted the decks all the time
of the engagement, neither gave the least mark of fear, except for their husbands."

Caraccioli was wounded in this engagement and was confined to his bed for two months.

By this time Misson and his men had collected such a vast
amount of gold and silver that they decided to settle down
permanently in the Far East and reap the rewards of their
adventures. They went to the Queen of Johanna and reminded her that they had been of great help to her in subduing her enemies. Misson requested that she furnish him with
three hundred men to help construct buildings on a point of
land which he had selected on the nearby coast of Madagascar. After a long debate with her counsellors the Queen
consented.

An old chronicle tells how the pirates went about constructing their colony: "The first thing they set about was
raising a fort on each side of the harbor, which they made of
an octagon figure. And having finished and mounted with
forty guns taken out of the Portuguese [ship] they raised
a battery of ten guns on an angle and began to raise houses
and magazines under the protection of their forts and ships.
The Portuguese was unrigged and all her sails and cordage
carefully laid up."

At the same time a party of pirates was sent into the interior to explore and discover if there were unfriendly natives in the vicinity. They found some natives but they seemed relatively harmless, for they were armed only with bows and arrows, so Captain Misson did not feel he was in any danger from the land. Although his fort was constructed of wood, he decided that it was sufficiently strong to defend his infant colony from the sea and land as well. He named the colony Libertatia.

Feeling secure, Misson set out on another cruise, for he needed more men to help settle his pirate colony. Soon he fell in with a Portuguese vessel mounting fifty guns and with a crew of three hundred. Instead of his boarding the Portuguese, the Portuguese promptly boarded Misson. But his men, expecting no quarter, fought so desperately that they soon cleared their decks of the enemy. Some even followed the Portuguese when they retreated to their own ship. Seeing his advantage, Misson led the rest of his men aboard, crying, "Death or victory!" During the mêlée, Misson and the Portuguese captain fought a furious duel with their cutlasses. Misson, being an expert swordsman, struck the captain such a powerful blow in the neck that he fell down the main hatch and died. That was the end of the fight, for, seeing their captain fall, the Portuguese sailors threw down their arms and called for quarter, which was granted.

This vessel was the second richest prize of Misson's career. She carried £200,000 in gold. Part of it had been transferred from her consort which had run ashore some time before.

On the way back to Libertatia with his prize, Misson sighted a strange sloop. When within cannon range she hoisted black colors and fired a gun to windward. To Misson, watching the little vessel through his spyglass from the poop of his heavily armed *Victoire*, this was sheer impudence. He brought his vessel into the wind, fired a gun to leeward, hoisted out a boat and prepared to board. Perceiving this, the sloop lay to. When Misson's lieutenant reached the stranger he found him to be Captain Tew, a native of Bermuda and like Misson, a sea rover. The French lieutenant told Tew about amiable Captain Misson and his pirate utopia of Libertatia. He invited Tew and his crew to become members of the colony.

Tew replied civilly that he could not give an answer until he had consulted his men. Meanwhile Misson drew closer to Tew's sloop and asked him to come aboard, promising to leave his lieutenant on the sloop as a hostage.

True to form, Misson royally entertained Tew aboard the *Victoire*. He described the pleasant life at Libertatia so graphically and persuasively that Tew was intrigued. He returned to his sloop and quickly convinced his men that they too should become citizens of Misson's republic. During the conversation between the two pirate captains aboard the *Victoire*, Captain Tew gave an account of his own life and exploits. He explained that he was born Thomas Tew and had followed the seas since he was a boy, going on many trading voyages between Bermuda and the West Indies. Some time before meeting with Captain Misson, he had received a letter of marque from Governor Richier of Bermuda, who instructed him to proceed to the west coast of Africa in company with Captain George Drew to harass the French. They were told to make the best of their way to the River Gambia and try to capture the French slave factory of Goory located there.

After leaving Bermuda, the two sloops kept company for some time but were separated by violent storms.

The more Captain Tew thought about his situation (in a small sloop alone on the wide Atlantic, with only the bare possibility of meeting his consort), the more dubious he became about the success of this venture. He called his men together and told them that although he had agreed to go on this expedition, it had been contrary to his judgment. He pointed out that even if it were successful, to use his own words, "It would be of no use to the public and only an advantage to a private company of men from whom we can expect no reward for our bravery. I can see nothing but danger in this undertaking without the least prospect of booty. I cannot suppose that any man is fond of fighting merely for fighting's sake. Few men venture their lives but with some view either of particular interest or public good. But I see neither in this venture. So, I say, let us turn our thoughts on how we may improve our circumstances. If you are so inclined I will undertake to shape a course which should lead us all to ease and plenty in which we may pass the rest of our days. One bold push will do our business and you may return home not only without danger but even with reputation."

These words met with immediate approval and they cried out, "A gold chain, or wooden leg, we'll stand by you!" This was the usual acknowledgment to a captain's proposition by Brothers of the Coast.

The next order of business, aboard Tew's sloop, was to choose a quartermaster. Although the rating of quartermaster was usually a minor one, among pirates he wielded influence second only to the captain's. As one historian remarked, "The quartermaster's opinion is like the Mufti's among the Turks. The captain can undertake nothing of which the quartermaster does not approve. We may say the quartermaster is a humble imitation of the Roman Tribune of the people; he speaks for and looks after the interest of the crew."

Once the decision to go a-roving was made, Tew shaped his course for the Cape of Good Hope, then steered for the Straits of Bab-el-Mandeb and the Red Sea.

Here Tew had beginner's luck. His sloop had hardly entered the inland sea when a tall ship hove over the horizon, bound from India to Arabia. Although he did not know it at that moment, she was richly laden and combined the functions of a merchant vessel with those of a man-o'-war. She carried instructions to clear the coast of rovers and was being followed by five more great vessels with the same orders. Aboard the flagship were some three hundred soldiers in addition to her crew of seamen.

The size of this great vessel did not intimidate Tew. Pointing a gnarled finger at her billowing canvas, he told his men that she carried their fortunes. With courage and skill they could take her. True, she carried a great number of guns. But he intended to board her with little loss, for it was well known that these Indian vessels took more care to run from danger than to exert themselves in the defense of their goods.

Tew made good his promise. Running under the stern of the flagship the pirates heaved grappling irons aboard, clambered up over the elaborately carved stern castle and swept the deck with pistol and cutlass.

Tew was not yet a veteran at the game of looting. Otherwise he would not have thrown overboard a great many bales of merchandise in his search for gold, silver and jewels. Apparently he had not heard of Messrs. Philipse, De Lancey, Van Cortlandt and other colonial merchants who would have been overjoyed to purchase the rich textiles and exotic East Indian products contained in the prize. Nevertheless, after removing all the powder and shot, which Tew needed, each man of his crew received precious metal and jewels to the value of £3000. In that day this amount was a veritable fortune.

Now Tew decided to strike while the iron was hot. He proposed to go searching for the other five ships, for he had been told by the officers of the prize that they were not far off. But here the quartermaster put in his oar and vehemently opposed the project. It was tempting fortune, he said, to take another large ship so easily. So most reluctantly, Tew ordered his sloop headed for Madagascar.

En route, the quartermaster again declared they should settle permanently on Madagascar, for the island was productive of all the necessities of life; the air was wholesome, the soil fruitful and the sea full of fish. This time the quartermaster was outvoted. Only twenty-three of the crew agreed to his idea. The rest declared themselves for Captain Tew, who had proposed that they should return to America. Again the ship's course was changed and she pointed her prow into the westering sun.

It was at this juncture that the *Victoire* hove in view and the two pirate captains met for the first time. As previously described, Captain Misson was more persuasive than Tew's quartermaster for now their vessels and the two prizes sailed for Misson's colony.

Tew's crew were impressed with the size and armament of Misson's fortifications which they saluted with nine guns and were answered with an equal number. Then followed days of celebration, carousing and feasting. The pirates who had remained ashore during the cruise of Captain Misson, headed by Captain Caraccioli (who now stumped along on a wooden leg), were glad to have their numbers strengthened by Tew's men and by the Portuguese prisoners Misson had taken, many of whom had decided to cast their lot with the pirates.

Those prisoners who refused to join the rovers, 137 in number, were allowed to depart in a captured sloop, well provisioned but with no armament. In return for this generosity the prisoners promised on their honor not to reveal the headquarters of the pirates or to send any vessels of war to harass them.

The next few years were peaceful and prosperous. Using Libertatia as a base, Tew, Misson and Caraccioli alternately went cruising, with good results. Apparently Thomas Tew fell under the spell of Misson and Caraccioli in their treatment of prisoners and slaves. On one occasion, after capturing an English slaver with 240 black men, women and boys aboard, Tew knocked off their chains and told them they were free.

The communal character of Misson's pirate colony is shown by his orders that there should be a common treasury where all booty was to be held and divided justly among the colonists. On one occasion a great quantity of English crowns was found aboard a Dutch East Indian galley. "These," says an old record, "were carried into the common treasury, money being of no use where everything was in common and no hedge bounded any particular man's property. The slaves Tew released in this cruise were employed in perfecting the dock and were treated on the footing of free people. They were not ignorant of the change in their condition and were therefore extremely diligent and faithful. A white man, or one of the old standing Negroes, wrought with every four, and made them understand the French words used in their works."

When it was Misson's turn to go roving, he also had his share of luck. Off the coast of Arabia Felix he fell in with a ship belonging to the Great Mogul, bound for Jidda with pilgrims for Mecca. The vessel was manned by Moorish mariners. The total number of people aboard was 1500, including the crew. Since this ship carried a heavy armament of 110 guns, it might be thought that she would have given a good account of herself. On the contrary, she made a very poor defense, especially because her decks were encumbered with bales and boxes and barrels of merchandise and the passengers often got in the way of the gun crews. Only a few shots were exchanged before Misson's resolute pirates clambered aboard. The Moors discharged one volley of small arms, then fled below decks.

Misson became the master of this great ship without the cost of a single man. It was obvious to him that his own ship could not travel far in company with such a crowded vessel, so he determined to set his prisoners ashore at Aden. But the crew raised a great howl when he told them that even the women would be set ashore. The pirates shouted that they wanted the women. Their clamor was so loud that Misson reluctantly agreed.

"This resolution was put in execution and they [the pirates] brought off a hundred girls from twelve to eighteen years old, who [had] designed to make the pilgrimmage [to Mecca] with their parents." So wrote Misson in his memoirs. The lamentations of the poor girls had such an effect upon Misson that he was for letting them go. But every one of his men was against him.

The voyage back to Libertatia was a difficult one. The East Indian ship was cumbersome and lumbering and a cranky sailer. When a violent storm arose, the vessel drifted dangerously toward shore and only by expert maneuvering was Misson able to save his prize. Eventually they returned home safely.

Now Misson had time properly to evaluate the great vessel. When he rummaged through her he was awestruck with the vast quantities of diamonds, rich silks, spices, Oriental carpets and raw gold she contained. After distributing the loot among his people, the vessel was broken up. Her fittings, metalwork and all useful gear were thriftily stored against future use aboard other pirate vessels. Her guns greatly strengthened the shore batteries.

By now the colony was firmly established with a large area of cultivated land and a quantity of pasturage supporting three hundred head of black cattle. Meanwhile the *Vic-*

toire, having grown old, was pulled to pieces and rebuilt, rerigged, victualed and made ready for sea.

Hardly had her bowsprit poked out of the harbor than she was driven back by five tall ships each mounting fifty guns and swarming with men. Here at last was the revenge for which Misson had been preparing. The alarm was sounded. All the pirates, including a hundred well-disciplined Negroes, were marshaled to repel the invaders. Misson and Caraccioli commanded the French contingents, while Tew captained the English.

Here is what happened, according to Captain Charles Johnson's narrative:

They stood directly fore the harbour with the Portuguese colors. They were warmly received by the two forts, which did not stop them, though it brought one of them on the careen [caused one to run ashore]. They entered the harbour and thought they had done their business but were saluted so warmly from the forts and batteries, sloops and ships, that two of them sunk outright and a great many men were drowned, though some of them got aboard the other ships. The Portuguese, who did not imagine they had been so well fortified, and thought in passing the two forts they should, without difficulty, land their men and easily root out this nest of Pirates, found now their mistake, for they durst not venture to hoist out a boat. They had wisely, however, contrived to enter just before the turn of the tide. Finding the attempt vain, and that they had lost a great many men, they clapped upon a wind, and with the help of the tide of ebb, made more haste out than they did to get in, leaving two of the ships sunk in the harbour. But they did not get off so cheaply, for no sooner were they clear of the forts, but Misson manning, with the utmost expedition, both the ships and the sloops, he gave them chase and engaged them at the mouth of the Bay. The Portuguese defended themselves with a great deal of gallantry and one of them put off the Libertatians twice, who boarded them from the two sloops. Two of them, finding themselves hard pressed, made a running fight and got off, and left the third to shift as well as he could.

One of the sloops and the *Victoire* fell upon the third, which defended itself until the decks ran with blood. A great number of the men were killed. Finding all resistance useless and that he was left to an unequal fight by his consorts, the Portuguese captain called for quarter. It was given both to his men and to himself. This prize yielded the pirates a great quantity of powder and shot.

"None of the prisoners was stripped and [as for] the officers, Misson, Caraccioli and Tew invited them to their tables, treating them very civilly and extolling the courage they had shown in their defense."

This battle gave ample evidence that the three pirate captains were not only resolute leaders, but also expert seamen and adept at outmaneuvering their enemies. It is also rather surprising, considering the quarrelsome nature of pirates, that Tew, an Englishman, and Misson, a Frenchman, got along so well together, especially since Misson was a Catholic and Tew a Protestant.

But shortly after the repulse of the Portuguese expedition, a quarrel did arise between Misson and his men and those belonging to Tew. Captain Tew recommended that the difficulty be settled by a champion being selected from each side who would engage the other in mortal combat with rapiers. Caraccioli was against it, alleging that such a decision "must necessarily be of damage to the public, since the brave men who fell, would be a weakening of their colony. He therefore desired Captain Tew to interpose the authority he had over his crew as he and Misson would endeavor to bring their men to an amicable agreement; and for the future, as this accident proved the necessity, wholesome laws should be made and a form of government entered upon."

This was the beginning of a remarkable republican government which united a crowd of seagoing outlaws who had the whole world for enemies.

After a meeting of the three commanders the next day, they assembled the colony and Misson addressed them: "Where there are no coercive laws, the weakest are always the sufferers and everything tends to confusion. Men's passions blind them to justice and make them ever partial to themselves. Therefore we ought to submit our differences to calm and disinterested persons who could examine and determine according to reason and equity who is in the right and who is in the wrong. We favor a democratical form where we ourselves are the makers and judges of our own laws."

The three commanders then asked their men to divide themselves into companies of ten men. Each company was to choose one to assist in setting up a form of government to make "wholesome laws for the good of the whole." They proposed that the treasure and cattle which they owned should be equally divided; also that any land that an individual would enclose with a fence should, in the future, be considered his property which no other could lay claim to. It was also determined to erect a great house of framed timbers wherein to meet for governmental purposes.

The structure was completed in the remarkably short time of two weeks because, says the old chronicle, "they had among them a great many who understood the handling of an axe." When the building was completed and the representatives of the groups of ten men were assembled (each group was called a State), Captain Caraccioli opened the session with an eloquent speech. He described the advantages to be derived from law and order and then emphasized the necessity of lodging supreme power in the hands of one individual. This man, he said, should be brave and virtuous and capable of punishing the vicious, according to the laws they were to establish. Such a power, he said, should not be for life nor be hereditary but terminate at the end of three years, at which time a new leader would be selected or the old one confirmed for another three years. By this means, he explained, the ablest men would always be at the head of affairs. The supreme ruler would have the title of Lord Conservator "and all the ensigns of royalty attend him."

The pirates approved all of Caraccioli's suggestions. Misson was unanimously chosen Conservator. He was to be addressed with the title of Supreme Excellence.

Apparently the pirates did not feel that any pressing matters needed to be decided by the meeting of the States, for it was determined that this body should meet only once a year. However, if the Conservator and his council felt it necessary for the common good, meetings would be called by him.

The first session of the States lasted ten days "and a great many wholesome laws were enacted, registered in the State book, printed and dispersed (for they had printers and letter-founders among them) and then the Conservator dissolved them."

Captain Thomas Tew received the title of Admiral, and Captain Caraccioli was made Secretary of State. This shrewd ex-priest chose a council of the ablest of the pirates without regard to their nationality or color or language. He supervised an equal division of booty and cattle, and everyone was pleased with the whole arrangement.

Admiral Tew was strongly in favor of building an arsenal and constructing additional vessels for their own protection, but was handicapped by the lack of men. The problem was that if all the able-bodied men in the colony were to be engaged in sea service, the farming projects would be neglected and the food supply seriously reduced. The truth was that Tew had begun to be restless and yearned to return to high seas robbery. He was soon granted permission to cruise in the *Victoire*.

He sailed for southern Madagascar and there enlisted a number of Englishmen who had settled on that coast of the big island. When he prepared to put out to sea again, some Englishmen, who had decided to remain ashore, urged him to put off his sailing and drink a bowl of punch with them. One bowl led to another and they all were so intent on their drinking that they did not realize the violence of a storm which had sprung up. Too late Captain Tew ran to the shore and made a signal for his boat to take him out to his ship. The sea ran so high that he could not get aboard. Then he had the sad experience of standing helpless and watching the *Victoire* drag her cables and drive ashore where she broke up. Her entire crew was drowned, for the place where she was swept was so high, precipitous and rocky that no one could save the men.

Now Captain Tew was virtually marooned on an isolated part of Madagascar with only a handful of fellow Englishmen. At the end of three months a large ship was sighted but took no notice of the pirates ashore. They built great fires to attract attention but to no avail. The ship sailed away. About a month later two sloops came in close and sent off a boat. In the stern sheets was the well-known figure of Captain Misson.

When Misson came ashore, he too told a tale of woe and tragedy. He related to Captain Tew that not long before, in the dead of night, two huge bands of natives crept upon sleeping Libertatia and slaughtered right and left before the startled pirates could defend themselves. Captain Caraccioli died bravely, trying to stem the fury of the natives.

Meanwhile Misson, fighting a courageous rearguard action, managed to get forty-five of his men on board two of the sloops. He was only able to salvage a quantity of rough diamonds and bar gold. He and his men were the sole survivors of the slaughter at Libertatia.

Then Captain Tew told Misson what had happened to him and about the disaster to the *Victoire*. He urged Misson to come with him to America where the Frenchman was unknown. With the riches he had salvaged he could set himself up as a gentleman of leisure. Misson consented. He divided the Englishmen and his own crew between the two sloops. He also generously shared his salvaged fortune with Tew, even giving a share to Tew's crew.

The two sloops went to sea and headed westward for the American colonies. Off Cape Infantes a great storm overtook the little vessels and they were in danger of foundering. One indeed was lost, carrying brave Captain Misson to his death, although a number of his crew survived and eventually reached France.[2]

Thanks to good luck and good seamanship, Tew survived the storm and made good his voyage to America without further incident. Thomas Tew landed in New York and, because of his wealth and hair-raising stories of adventure, became a crony of the rascally Governor Fletcher. Early colonial records refer to this friendship and when Fletcher was questioned in London he stated that he was well impressed with this "privater."

Tew settled in Newport, Rhode Island. Soon stories of his exploits in the Red Sea spread about town. The whole community was fascinated and excited by his tales of vast treasures looted from the ships of the Great Mogul. The news of his exploits spread along the Atlantic coast. Everyone soon knew about the "mighty mass of money" he had brought with him. It was estimated at £10,000. This of course was a relatively small sum compared with what he had amassed before the *Victoire* foundered. What he brought to Newport was merely what generous Captain Misson had given him.

While Thomas Tew's vessel lay in the harbor at Newport, an eyewitness reported that "servants from most places of the country [came] running from their masters, sons from their parents and many had their children and relations going a-roving against their wills—many was the young man went out—whereof some returned and many yet out which are better dead or dead in law so that they durst not return to their native country and relations."

It was almost like the California gold rush a hundred and fifty years later. Young men of good families pleaded to sign aboard Tew's vessel. Lads deserted their homes, begging to serve as cabin boys, while preachers and parents bellowed against this evil man and his ill-gotten gains.

Meanwhile Tew had not forgotten the owners of the Bermuda sloop in which he had set forth on an expedition to the coast of West Africa. He wrote and sent them money amounting to fourteen times the value of their vessel.

No one in Rhode Island or New York made any effort to prosecute Tew as a pirate at this time. It was probably because he claimed he had looted only vessels belonging to the Great Mogul. The truth is he had also robbed a number of English ships. But with such slow communications in those days he had not yet been posted as a pirate in London.

"Captain Tew lived unquestioned etc. He had an easy fortune and designed to live quietly at home," says an old chronicle. But his reputation had now expanded to great size. He was besieged by many members of his old crew who had squandered their shares of loot and were hungry for more, not to mention the hundreds of adventurous men who wanted to go to the Red Sea also.

At last the old urge overcame Tew's better judgment and he agreed to set out on another voyage. He bought a small sloop and with a picked crew of veterans and some others, entered the Red Sea. Just as in the old days, a ship belonging to the Great Mogul of India hove in sight. This time Tew's luck deserted him. In the fight that followed, a round shot struck him in the belly and ripped away his bowels which he tried to push back into his torn body with his hands. There was no one aboard like Misson or Caraccioli to take over the leadership and the pirates were so terrified at Tew's horrible end that they surrendered and were made prisoners by the Hindus. What happened to them is unknown. It is likely that they were tortured to death.

So ended the career of Thomas Tew, who tossed away the opportunity to live out his days as a wealthy "gentleman" in the colony of Rhode Island. The old lure of a blue sea, a fair wind and a richly laden ship was too much for his adventurous soul.

Captain Kidd on the quarterdeck of the Adventure Galley, *anchored in New York harbor on the eve of sailing in search of the Red Sea Men. (From the painting by Howard Pyle.)*

8

William Kidd,
Merchant Captain

In 1695 New York was a town with a population of between four and five thousand souls, with a splendid harbor and an active trade with the mother country. There was also an active trade in firewater with the Indians upcountry in exchange for pelts and much land-grabbing. But far more excitement and thirst for adventure were whipped up by the profitable activities of the Red Sea Men. Everyone was hungry for riches at the expense of the Great Mogul. Piracy was accepted with complacency and even with enthusiasm. Freebooters swaggered down the streets, drank and caroused in the taverns and tossed gold and silver about with abandon.

The exploits of Captains Avery and Tew had fired the imaginations of almost everyone in the colonies and had sent young adventurers swarming aboard pirate vessels demanding to sign on for a trip to Madagascar. A man could make his fortune by a single voyage. It has been estimated that, at the Port of New York alone, four hundred pirates congregated when the ships were in. There were several hundred massed in Providence, Rhode Island, planning a trip to the Red Sea.

Auctions of pirate loot were common. The eastern end of Long Island was a favorite meeting place for pirates and smugglers, who had no difficulty in shipping their goods across Long Island Sound to Stamford and New Haven. From there it was transported by carts to New York, Boston and Philadelphia.

Even Samuel Sewall, a respected Boston judge, operated a private mint in Boston to which the pirates brought their Arabian gold and silver coins to be melted down and converted into more respectable currency.

Yet in the midst of all the noise, confusion and money-making, there was beginning to develop a strong opposition to this free and easy way of life and demands for its end. In London a number of broadsides were printed and distributed describing the scandalous conditions caused by piracy and a rascally governor of New York. It was the public out-cry on both sides of the Atlantic that stirred the Lords of Trade to investigate Fletcher and finally dismiss him.

Although Governor Fletcher did not know it at this time, his successor was going to be the Earl of Bellomont, who would take office as Captain-General of the Province of Massachusetts Bay and Governor of New York. Born Richard Coote, he succeeded his father as an Irish baronet. He had been a warm supporter of the Prince of Orange and was on a friendly footing with him when he became King William III. In March 1689, he had been created Earl of Bello-mont in the Irish peerage and given extensive grants of land.

By appointing Bellomont to the most important colonial

post in America, the Crown at last recognized the urgency for having a responsible, honest and hard-working Governor. What was needed was a more unified conduct of the affairs of the English plantations on the northern frontier of the American continent, particularly in matters of defense. Scarcely less pressing were the problems presented by the utter disregard of the imperial trade laws by colonial merchants and shipowners and their connivance with the pirates of the Red Sea and Caribbean.

Bellomont did not immediately take up his duties as Governor. He remained in England and Ireland for nearly a year putting his affairs in order. During this time he was told by the Lords of Trade about the malfeasance of Governor Fletcher, and of the corrupt character of New York officials and merchants and the growing impudence of the Red Sea Men. Although he did not dream of it at this time, Lord Bellomont was about to become embroiled in an affair that was to have a shattering impact on himself and many others (prominent as well as notorious), touch off an explosive political wrangle, and cause a celebrated trial which ended with three men dangling at the end of a hangman's noose. It was an affair which had elements of drama scarcely rivaled on the stage, each episode accurately recorded in official government documents in America and England. As in most true-life dramas, *Chance* played an important role, along with *Bad Luck, Poor Judgment, Deceit, Lying* and *Stupidity*.

It all started with Robert Livingston (often spelled Livingstone in letters and official papers). He was a Scot, a person of "considerable estate and fair reputation," who divided his time between New York and Albany. In 1695 Livingston made a voyage to England. He had several reasons for going. As Commissioner of Indian Affairs and a member of the New York Council, he had loaned money to the provincial government before and during Governor Fletcher's administration. He had never been repaid. There were also certain accounts to be settled with his London agents that could not be satisfactorily adjusted by correspondence. Furthermore, Livingston wanted a voice in the decision regarding the legality of the administration of Captain Jacob Leisler, who had taken over the functions of Governor in New York during the time of confusion in 1688 when the Stuarts were ejected forever from the throne of England. Livingston's final reason for coming to London was to prod the government into taking action against the Red Sea Men and their illegal trade.

Livingston was shrewd, imaginative, opportunistic, and reasonably honest, according to the morality of the times. During the considerable period he spent in London, he was well aware of the howls of the East India Company for assistance in protecting their precious convoys in the Red Sea and Indian Ocean. He had also heard much talk about the emissaries of the Great Mogul who were pestering His Majesty to wipe out piracy. But His Majesty had retorted somewhat testily that he had a war with the French on his hands and could not spare even one man-o'-war to go pirate chasing.

If the King could not supply a vessel of the Royal Navy, Livingston reasoned, there was another way of accomplishing the thing. Excitedly his agile mind began to work upon a scheme—a scheme that would knock over two birds with a single stone: destroy the pirates on the one hand and line the pockets of a syndicate of respectable men. The plan was simplicity itself: organize a group of wealthy and influential individuals who would put up sufficient money to buy, equip and man a privately armed vessel. The captain would carry the King's commission to hunt down and destroy pirates operating in East Indian waters. Livingston was confident that he could persuade a select and titled group to invest in his scheme and with their influence secure a Royal commission.

The crew of the pirate-chasing vessel would be compensated according to the time-honored principle of "no purchase [booty] no pay." The backers of the enterprise would, of course, receive handsome dividends on their investment, in addition to a return of their capital, provided the merchandise and treasure taken from the pirates proved as great as expected. Livingston had no doubt whatever that it would.

Yet, strangely, it never seemed to occur to him or any of his syndicate that they would be receiving booty consisting of stolen goods—loot taken from legitimate East Indian merchants and even British subjects. It was as if a Chief of Police and several of his friends personally bought a squad car, hired a policeman-driver and some other police officers and told them to pursue, overtake and capture a gang of bank robbers. The hired officers would be paid according to the amount of money taken from the robbers. If they failed to capture them, they got nothing. But the Police Chief and his friends would get the lion's share of the money stolen from the bank, if a capture was made, and the bank would be out of luck.

The big question in Livingston's mind, once he began working on his plan, was: who was the mariner honest enough and capable enough and courageous enough to command the pirate-hunting expedition and see that it paid off?

Not long afterwards, in August 1695, Livingston fell in with Captain William Kidd of New York, who was visiting London. It was a chance meeting, for Livingston and three of his friends, Philip French, William Carter and Giles Shelley, were on their way to attend divine services at a Presbyterian church in Chelsea. Livingston's friendship with

Shelley is significant. This man was soon to become a notorious pirate-trader who would take a floating arsenal of cannon, muskets, pistols, powder and ball to the pirates of Madagascar and return to New York loaded with money, slaves and stolen merchandise.

There were cordial greetings between Livingston and his friends and Captain Kidd. Livingston recorded in his journal that he took "Kidd with me to sleep at my house, because he was so far from his lodgings." What went on that night between the influential colonial merchant and the seemingly honest and respectable merchant captain, William Kidd, is unknown. But it is almost a certainty that they discussed Livingston's scheme.

These two men had been friends in New York. They were fellow Scotsmen. Kidd had sided with Livingston in the Leisler controversy. It is not difficult to conjecture that Robert Livingston soon decided that Captain William Kidd was precisely the man he was looking for to command a pirate-chasing vessel, privately owned and operated.

In the light of all the known facts surrounding the Red Sea Men at this time, the great number of ships and men they commanded, their heavily fortified bases at Madagascar and St. Mary, and their wide area of operation in the Eastern Seas, it seems incredible that Livingston and Kidd and the Lords of Trade and Bellomont and even the King could believe that a single ship, even though heavily armed and with a crew of 150, could possibly make more than a slight dent in the pirate trade. Yet no one raised this point. Was the proposed expedition, then, merely an excuse for a syndicate of allegedly honest men to conspire to fill their purses with Arabian gold and silver and precious gems, safeguarded by a semblance of legality? The events that followed will enable the reader to judge for himself.

Now let us have a look at this William Kidd and his background.[1] Kidd's origin is obscure. Most authorities believe that he was born in Scotland in 1645. There is a tradition that his father was a Presbyterian minister. Kidd followed the sea and became sufficiently skilled to command his own merchant vessel out of the Port of New York. Over the years he seems to have built a reputation as a respectable citizen and was regarded as a skilled and honest mariner.

In 1691 when a pirate was cruising off the coast of Massachusetts, Kidd was sent by provincial officials to hunt down the sea rover. Apparently he drove the pirate away, although there is no record of a capture.

At this time England and France were at war and English privateers were active again in the Caribbean. Kidd sailed under a letter of marque and was so successful in this venture that the Assembly at Albany awarded him £150 for his services.

In the spring of 1691 Kidd married Mrs. Sarah Bradley Cox Oort, a wealthy widow who owned a number of pieces of valuable property in New York. Kidd added several purchases of his own. This was an era of real estate speculation and Kidd was highly successful, for his property occupied ground now bordering on such well-known streets of lower Manhattan as Pearl, Pine, Wall, and Water. His home was a handsome brick structure on the corner of Hanover and Pearl Streets. His drawing room was the talk of the town when he exhibited a beautiful "Turkey carpet," said to be the first of its kind in America. So here we have the picture of an apparently sober, substantial citizen of the Port of New York who not only owned a town house but also had a summer place out in the country in Harlem.[2]

Kidd's friends were equally respectable, if not distinguished. He had been on familiar terms with three governors in succession. He was acquainted with most of the leading merchants and landowners, including Robert Livingston.

But what the good people of New York did not know was that Kidd had hobnobbed with pirates during his privateering days in the West Indies. This was verified by testimony given in London five months after Kidd's death by the notorious pirate Robert Culliford. This man declared that he had "Sayled in a ship called the *Blessed William*, Captain William Kidd, Commander, out of ffalmouth harbour, in the island of Antegoa [Antigua, B.W.I.] which ship had been a ffrench privateer and was run away by Collover [Culliford], Kidd and five or six more and then carried into Antegoa." While Kidd was ashore, Collover and Samuel Burgess [another famous piratical character] stole the ship and, with eighteen or twenty men for a crew, set out for the East Indies.

One of the main reasons why Livingston wanted Kidd to command the ship supplied by his syndicate was his knowledge of those pirates, their methods and their haunts. Culliford further testified that "Captain William Kidd, lately come from New York [to England] in a Sloop of his own upon the account of Trade . . . told him [Livingston] he knew most of the principal men who had been abroad roving, and divers who were lately gone out, and likewise had some knowledge of the places where they usually made their rendezvous . . . He said tho' the Pirates were many in number, yet they had at that time no Ships of considerable force."[3]

Whether Kidd actually made these statements to Livingston during their talks about his scheme or whether Livingston already knew of Kidd's Caribbean experiences is unknown. It is likely that Livingston knew a good deal about Kidd's past and used it as an argument to persuade Kidd to command the venture.

Did Kidd actually engage in acts of piracy in the Caribbean? There is good reason to believe so. Even the respectable captain of a privateer, ostensibly cruising against the French, could instantly transform himself into a pirate if the prey was rich enough and worth the risk. It would have been a simple matter to toss the crew of the captured ship to the sharks and sink or burn the vessel, which would then join hundreds of others that left port never to return. It is also probable that the proceeds of Kidd's cruises against the French as a privateer included a considerable quantity of illegal loot. Evidence of this is found in a letter from Richard Oglethorp, a businessman of South Carolina. Although this letter was written five years after Kidd was hanged, it accused Kidd of trading with Danish merchants of the Island of St. Thomas[4] who at the same time were trading with the French. At this period the Island of St. Thomas was a notorious rendezvous for smugglers, illicit traders and pirates.

A little more than two weeks after Livingston first met Kidd in London, the New York merchant's claims for reimbursement of moneys owed him by the Crown were taken up by the Lords of Trade. Kidd was one of the witnesses in his favor. So was the unsavory Giles Shelley. The case dragged on until January 2, 1696, when Livingston was awarded most of the money he claimed, together with confirmation of his office as Secretary of Indian Affairs.

Meanwhile Livingston had been busy organizing his syndicate. He had been working hard on Kidd to take command of the ship. Kidd had been reluctant. Was he afraid that his past might be embarrassingly revealed when he hailed his old pirate cronies into court? Or perhaps, knowing his own unstable character, he was not sure he could play the part of a tough pirate-killer. Livingston assured Kidd that he would have full protection, come what may.

Moreover, he would sail under a Royal Commission especially drawn for hunting pirates. Here is Kidd's own description of Livingston's high-pressure methods. It was written in Boston in 1699 as an "Instrument of Protest," an effort to clear himself of charges of piracy after he returned from the expedition:

> Livingstone [sic] a merchant of Albany carried me to wait on my Lord Bellomont at his house in Dover Street, where both my Lord and Livingstone urged me with many arguments to accept the command of this ship under the King's Commission ... I pressed to be excused to pursue my voyage to New York, whereupon Lord Bellomont added threats to his wheedles, and told me I should not be allowed to carry my own ship out of the river of Thames unless I accepted command of this ship ... Livingstone carried me to the house of the Duke of Shrewsbury, the Lord Chancellor, Earl of Romney and Admiral Russel ... where he discoursed them, but would not suffer me to see or speake to them ... Lord Bellomont assured me again and again that the noble lords would stifle all complaints in England and he in New York, and would condemn all goods brought in by me, and dispose of them privately ... He gave me to my Lord Bellomont, the character of a bold and hardy man. I thinking myself safe with a King's commission and the protection of so many great men, owners, accepted, thinking that it was in my Lord Bellomont's power, as governor of New York to oppress me if I still continued obstinate ... Before I went to sea, I waited twice on my Lord Romney and Admiral Russell (now Lord Orford). Both hastened me to sea, and promised to stand by me in all my undertakings.

It is unlikely that Bellomont made any such threats. No doubt Kidd was overawed by his Lordship's imperious manner and could not help thinking that Bellomont *could* make it extremely hard for him if he chose.

That Livingston was overjoyed at the outcome is reflected in his journal: "The other matter, of Kid, has also given me much trouble, and at last, this evening . . . I discussed this matter with two great personages and satisfied them. They take the Earl of R—— into partnership and they are now four in number[5] and the business is to proceed. I hope by this means my affaire may have a happy ending." Could this last sentence be interpreted to mean that he hoped Kidd would sail home loaded to the gunwales with rich booty, which would further enhance Livingston's fortune?

A week after these lines were written an agreement between Kidd, Livingston and Bellomont was signed and sealed. On behalf of his Whig backers (none of whose names appeared on the documents), Bellomont undertook to pay three quarters of the cost of buying, provisioning, outfitting and arming the vessel. Kidd and Livingston agreed to underwrite the remainder. Bellomont agreed to secure a properly worded Royal commission for Kidd from His Majesty. To protect his investment, canny Bellomont required Kidd to sign a bond for £20,000 and Livingston a bond for £10,000 as guarantees that they would fulfill their obligations.

The Earl also inserted a provision that in case Kidd did not capture any pirates or their cargoes, Bellomont was to be repaid for his capital investment before March 25, 1697. There was also a provision that if Kidd was lucky and brought in booty valued at £100,000 or more, the Earl and Livingston would be awarded the *Adventure Galley* as a bonus. Individual shares of Kidd and Livingston were to be one tenth of the whole. In case of the death of either, the amounts were to be awarded to their heirs. The King's commission to Kidd was impressive.* It was decorated with

---

* The King's commission to William Kidd is given in full in the Appendix, page 210.

elaborate scrollwork and flourishes, with an engraving of His Majesty in the upper left-hand corner, and was couched in the flowery language of the day and sealed with the Great Seal:

> *William Rex.*
> William the Third, by the grace of God,
> King of England, Scotland, France and Ireland,
> Defender of the Faith etc.
> > To our trusty and well-beloved
> > Captain William Kid,
> > Commander of the ship *Adventure Galley* . . .
> > Greeting . . .

His Majesty had never laid eyes on this man. As was routine in such matters, the King was taking the word of his petitioners, Bellomont & Company, that Kidd was "trusty and well beloved." Kidd was extremely proud of this commission and took pleasure in showing it to all and sundry.

The commission contained two significant orders, neither of which Kidd later obeyed: (1) He was to keep an exact journal of his proceedings, together with a list of pirates captured. (2) He was strictly charged (as he was to answer the contrary to his peril) that he would not offend or molest any of England's friends or allies, their ships or subjects.

In addition to the King's commission, Kidd was given another which was called a Commission of Reprisals. Since England and France were at war, this commission authorized him to capture French merchant ships if he should meet any. But his chief mission was to hunt down and capture the Red Sea Men and their ships and cargoes.

Captain William Kidd was now ready for the Great Pirate Hunt. He had a new ship of 284 tons, mounting thirty-four guns, named the *Adventure Galley*. Kidd sincerely believed in his mission, and selected his officers and men with great care. They were good honest English seamen, mostly family men. But he was shorthanded, for his total crew comprised only eighty sailors, which was far less than a full complement for a privateer of this size. Yet all seemed well.

It was May of 1696. The weather was favorable. After farewells had been said to Bellomont & Company, Kidd got under weigh. Scarcely had he cleared the Thames than he was ordered to heave to by a signal from H.M.S. *Duchess*. A small boat arrived with a message from Captain Stuart, brought by a young lieutenant who lined up the crew of the *Adventure Galley* and pressed most of them into the Royal Navy. The vigorous protests of Captain Kidd were ignored. The pressed seamen were taken aboard the *Duchess* and that was the last Kidd saw of them. He angrily went ashore and registered a strong objection with the Admiralty. Instead of giving him back his own men, he was sent human scum—jailbirds, criminals, and thieves of the lowest sort.

There was a delay of nineteen days before he got this miserable crew and it was not until July 4 that the *Adventure Galley* arrived in New York. Kidd's slow start was somewhat compensated for by the capture of a French prize en route. This ship was condemned by an Admiralty court, legal receipts given, and the Governor's share of one fifteenth and the King's share of one tenth of the proceeds of the sale of ship and cargo were duly forwarded.

Historians have speculated (not without reason) how Kidd occupied his time in New York between July and September of 1696. Why did he tarry there for more than two months? One probable reason was that he was busy supervising the construction of a handsome mansion. No doubt he expected to return home with a shipload of treasure and pass the remainder of his years in comfort and luxury in his new home. Other authorities claim that he spent most of his time carousing in the taverns with his cronies. This is less likely, for he had a local reputation to maintain and it is hardly to be supposed that he would quickly turn from a sober merchant captain into a rollicking rumpot.

At all events he did not hurry to embark on his cruise. Part of the time he was busy enlisting additional men to fill out his full complement.

The news that Captain Kidd was about to set forth against the pirates of the Red Sea spread through the provinces like a grass fire. Young men with no experience but with an eye to adventure and Arabian gold clamored to be signed on. There were others too, men with mahogany complexions, with crow's-feet about their eyes from squinting into the tropic sun, who wore gold earrings and walked with a roll, who gruffly demanded a berth in Kidd's foc'sle. The *Adventure Galley* at last set sail on September 6, 1696.

Governor Fletcher, still in office, but soon to be replaced by Bellomont, was even at this late hour allowing known pirates to escape the law. Blandly he wrote to the Lords of Trade:

> . . . the crew of one Coates (a Red Sea pyrate) threw over a great deal of East India goods and most of them separated and left the ship at the East End of the Island of Nassau [Long Island] when I heard of it I call'd the Councill, who advised that the ship be brought to New York. The men were pardoned under an act offering pardon to the pyrates . . . It may be my unhappiness but not my crime if they turn pyrates. I have heard of none yet that have done so.

Precisely what act of pardon Fletcher referred to is obscure. If it was an act passed by his own Council, it was illegal, for no one had the right to pardon pirates except

King William himself through an Act of Grace issued over His Majesty's signature.

In the same letter to the Lords of Trade, Fletcher referred to Captain Kidd's sailing. He voices doubt about Kidd's ability to control his motley crew aboard the *Adventure Galley:*

> One Captain Kidd lately arrived here and produced a Commission under the Great Seal of England for suppressing of pyrates, when he was here many flockt to him from all parts, men of desperate fortunes, and necessitous in expectation of getting vast treasure, he sailed from hence with 150 men as I am inform'd a great part of them are from this province. It is generally believed here, they will have money *pr.fas aut nefas*, that if he mises of the design intended, for which he had commission, 'twill not be in Kidd's power to govern such a hord of men under no pay.

Confirmation of Fletcher's doubts came all too soon.

There is a legend that Captain Kidd buried his Bible before turning pirate. No evidence has come to light that he ever did so, as shown in this old print. Inset is the signature of Captain William Kidd.

9

William Kidd, Pirate

LORD BELLOMONT did not arrive to take up his duties in New York until a year and seven months after Kidd had sailed from that port, en route to the East Indies. His voyage to America was long and stormy. It was an omen of his career as Governor. Though honest, the Earl was not especially well fitted to deal with the complicated affairs of the colonies at that time. He was high spirited and energetic, but prone to quick judgments, followed by action. He lacked the deliberate prudence and capacity for indirect methods that characterize a good politician and an able administrator. Bellomont also lacked experience in governing and did not thoroughly investigate certain matters as deeply as he should. This was particularly true in the case of William Kidd. He took Livingston's word that Kidd was honest and able and let it go at that. If the Earl had delved into Kidd's past, he might not have been so enthusiastic about the captain's capacity for chasing pirates.

Things went badly almost from the moment of Bellomont's arrival in New York on April 2, 1698. He received a cold reception from the "Gentlemen of the Councill," most of whom had been cronies of Fletcher.

"None offered me any assistance in the Government, [he complained in his first letter to the Lords of Trade.[1] The Council spread false rumors] whereby men's minds are disturbed and an odium cast upon the Government. These Gentlemen of the Councill, by drawing back, endeavour to make the Government uneasy for me. [Fletcher's administration had put His Majesty's affairs] so out of frame that it will cost me more pain and trouble to bring them into order and to support the dignity of His Majesty's Government and the just observance of his laws. The carelessness and corruption of the officers of the revenue and customes have been so great for some years past that although the trade of this place hath been four times as much as formerly and the city greatly enlarged and inriched yet His Majesty's revenues arising from the customes hath decreased the one half from what it was ten years since; and the merchants here have been so used to unlawful trade that they were almost ready to mutiny on some seizures I caused to be made (a few days after I landed) on Goods imported in the ship *Fortune* commanded by Captain Maston and it was with the greatest unwillingness and backwardness that His Majesty's collector, Mr. Chidley Brooke did make this seizure, who told me that it was none of his business . . . that he had no boat, and other excuses; and when I gave him positive commands to do it, which he could not avoid, yet his delay of four days time gave opportunity to the ship wholly to unload a rich cargo of East India goods, believed to be worth twenty thousand pounds; and only the last boatloads from her were seized to the value of one thousand pounds . . .

I shall take the best and most speedy methods I can for the Just observance of the Acts of Trade . . . but I shall have small assistance from the Gentelemen of his Majesty's Councill, because they are most of them Merchants, and several of themselves the persons concerned in the breach of these laws. . .

Bellomont was learning fast. He reported New York to be a "nest of Pirates," with ships fitted out from that port with commissions as privateers. He also informed their Lordships of the great trade between New York and Madagascar "from whence great quantities of East India goods are brought, which are certainly purchased from pirates." (As if their Lordships didn't already know!)

Bellomont also delved into the matter of the commissions issued by Fletcher to Tew, Glover, Hoare and others. He quickly found out what everyone else in town already knew, that, although the commissions appeared to have been given only against the King's enemies, the captains who held them were actually bound for a wild spree of looting the Great Mogul's ships. The Earl also discovered that the bonds given by those rogues were fraudulent and issued with the connivance of Fletcher's own private secretary, Daniel Honon. He had blotted out his name in the body of the bonds, then had removed his signature and torn off his own seal in an effort to conceal his connection with the fraud.

Meanwhile a rising tide of resentment on the part of the mercantile community was lapping at Bellomont's door. "They say," he wrote to the Lords of Trade, "I have ruined the Town by hindering the privateers (for so they call the pirates) from bringing in £100,000 since my coming."

Matters got so bad that bloodshed was barely avoided. When Bellomont sent his officers to seize certain goods illegally landed, "a tumult of the Merchants was made and the said officers were locked up and imprisoned for three hours . . . and the officers were in danger of being murdered; I thereupon sent the Lieutenant Governor and three files of men [soldiers] with my servants who broke open the doors and freed the officers and assisted them in carrying the goods seized to the customs house."

Now we will leave Governor Bellomont and his troubles temporarily, and return to the *Adventure Galley*, which had cleared Sandy Hook on September 6, 1696. There were two men on board who were going to make trouble for Kidd: Samuel Bradley, his honest but bad-tempered brother-in-law, and William Moore, the gunner. There is little doubt that Moore had been a pirate, as his later actions testify. In any case he was a stirring stick among the crew and Kidd determined to keep a watchful eye on him.

The first landfall of the *Adventure Galley* was the island of Madeira, where Kidd bought wine and some provisions. He then sailed to Bona Vista, one of the Cape Verde Islands, where he took on some salt.

After Kidd rounded the Cape of Good Hope, he sighted a large convoy on the horizon. The vessels were identified as those of the English East India Company. Kidd made himself known to Captain Warren, commodore of the three men-of-war that were guarding the convoy. Witnesses later testified that the *Adventure Galley* kept company with the convoy for six days. Commodore Warren was suspicious. He thought that Kidd's crew had a hangdog look and did not act like peaceful merchant seamen. Meanwhile, when Kidd was entertained by the officers of the flagship, he got drunk and boasted about what he was going to do when he reached the Red Sea; how many pirates he was going to capture and hang; and about the shipload of treasure he was going to take back.

Captain Warren was short of men and asked Kidd to supply a few. Kidd, in an expansive mood, promised him thirty hands. But the following night Kidd sneaked away from the convoy and sailed over the horizon without keeping his promise.

A stop was made at Johanna in the Comore Islands on the east coast of Africa. Here his men acted very much the way they used to do in Jamaica after a pirate raid. They caroused ashore, attacked the inhabitants, and behaved in a most disgraceful manner. This incident gives a clue to Kidd's later troubles: he was unable to control his men or to exert the strict discipline necessary to keep such an unruly crowd in hand.

To add to Kidd's troubles, when the vessel arrived at Madagascar, he discovered that all the pirate vessels operating out of St. Mary and other ports were away at sea looking for prizes. This was a keen disappointment to Kidd and his crew. It would mean days and weeks of searching and there was no telling where the pirate ships might be.

Then another blow fell. An epidemic of cholera swept through the ship taking the lives of a third of the crew. There is no record of their names, but it is probable that more of the London scum died than the others. There was a growing agitation to go cruising and either hunt down the freebooters or go a-pirating on their own account. But there was a further delay. The *Adventure Galley* had sprung several leaks which had to be repaired before putting to sea. Urged on by his crew, Kidd hurried repairs, took on water and provisions and set sail for the Malabar Coast. He arrived there in June, four months after reaching Madagascar.

For a long time the *Adventure Galley* cruised up and down the Malabar Coast, capturing neither pirates nor French vessels. When again the ship needed provisions and repairs, Kidd had no money. He had spent it all in Madagascar, preparing the ship for this voyage. He was fortunate in borrowing a sum of money from some merchants to supply his ship with food and make the necessary repairs. All the while his crew were grumbling and demanding action. So far they had captured nothing. The pressure was more than Kidd could stand. He had resisted temptation several times when ships of the Great Mogul had passed by, practically begging to be taken. One can well imagine the sour-faced crew leaning over the bulwarks of the *Adventure Galley*, staring hungrily at the rich Indian vessels as they disappeared over the horizon.

Kidd began his unlawful career by robbing several small ships. The crew demanded bigger and better prizes. He could resist them no longer. The pirate chaser now became a pirate himself.

Kidd's situation was also aggravated by the desertion of a number of his men who left him to seek better fortunes elsewhere. Later, when they came to testify against him, they claimed that they left Kidd because they were unwilling to turn pirate!

Since the pickings had been so poor on the Malabar Coast, Kidd decided to sail for the Red Sea. He touched at a port near the entrance to the Red Sea and robbed the natives of corn. By this time he was fully determined to throw off his mask of respectability and play the role of a tough sea rover. He called his crew together and he told them that they were now going pirating. He said that the Mocha Fleet, a rich Indian convoy, was due to sail their way. Later he was quoted as saying, "We have been unsuccessful hitherto, but courage, boys, we will make our fortunes out of this fleet."

The *Adventure Galley* anchored off Bab's Key at the entrance of the Red Sea. Kidd sent a boat along the coast to see if they could pick up any news of the Mocha Fleet. To their joy the spies returned declaring that they had seen fourteen or fifteen ships ready to set sail from a nearby port, some with English, some with Dutch, and some with Moorish colors. This was according to an international convoy plan designed for mutual protection against pirates.

Four days later at dusk the great fleet hove over the horizon. Through his spyglass Kidd identified an English and a Dutch man-of-war. The rest were "Moorish." This term was loosely applied to Arabian vessels and Indian vessels. Seamen in those days considered anyone with a dusky skin to be a "Moor."

When the fleet came within a mile or two of the *Adventure Galley,* Kidd hoisted English colors to make them think he was a merchantman wishing to join the convoy. Apparently he was accepted as such, for he fell in line in the very center of the convoy. Then he did what seems a very foolish thing. He opened fire on a Moorish ship which was running parallel to his own. The whole convoy was alarmed and one of the men-of-war bore down on Kidd and opened fire. Heavily outgunned, Kidd turned tail and ran.

This piece of stupidity is really amazing. An experienced pirate would have never done such a thing. He would have waited until one of the ships dropped behind the convoy. Then he too would have dropped behind, ostensibly to render aid and, when the convoy was over the horizon, would have attacked and captured the vessel. This was standard practice in the Caribbean. Any first-class pirate would have been shocked at Kidd's amateur tactics.

Kidd now headed again for the Malabar Coast. His first prize was a small vessel from Aden. This was a Moorish vessel, but the captain was an Englishman named Parker. The only other European aboard was a Portuguese called Don Antonio. Kidd forced these two men to join him, on pain of death. Parker, who knew the coast well, was made pilot. The Portuguese acted as interpreter. Their agreement to join Kidd came only after they had been badly treated. A contemporary record declares that he caused them to be "hoisted up by the arms and drubbed with a naked cutlass, to force them to discover whether they had any money on board [their own vessel] . . . But as they had neither gold nor silver on board, he got nothing by his cruelty; however, he took from them a bale of pepper and a bale of coffee." Small pickings indeed!

Even though Kidd's prize was insignificant, the news spread quickly along the coast. When Kidd touched at a port called Carawar, several English merchants at that place came on board and demanded that Kidd give up Parker and the Portuguese. Kidd denied that he knew any such persons, for he had hidden them away in the hold, where they were kept for seven or eight days and were only released after Kidd left port.

By this time, the Malabar Coast had really become alarmed by Kidd's actions. A Portuguese man-of-war was ordered to cruise against him. Kidd, overtaken, turned and fought. The action lasted six hours. Kidd battled stubbornly, but his enemy was larger and more powerful. Again Kidd turned and ran.

Why did Kidd turn pirate? What were the psychological and material factors that brought him to this dangerous decision? We will never really know, of course. But it is interesting to explore his motives and do a bit of speculation. In the first place, Lord Bellomont, while honest and eager to suppress piracy, was ignorant of its far-reaching character in the Red Sea area and naïve about his own and Kidd's ability to stamp it out. Certainly Kidd must have realized that a single ship of forty guns would be unable to successfully fight and capture more than one or two pirate ships of equal size and weight of metal. At this time it would have taken virtually the entire English navy to stamp out piracy in the Red Sea area, concentrating on English pirates alone. Even if all these had been captured, there were large numbers of French corsairs, Dutch sea rovers, and pirates of other nationalities to deal with. This may have been one reason why Kidd at first refused to take on the assignment. But, being pressed, he may have figured that he would make a brave show of chasing pirates, loot peaceful ships on his own account, and then return home and brazen it out, gambling on his previously "good" record.

Kidd's contention that he was forced into piracy by a disgruntled and threatening crew of former pirates scarcely holds water. It is true that he was a poor disciplinarian and lacked the hard, ruthless fighting spirit which characterized the most successful sea rovers. Yet to enforce stern discipline was not an impossible task. A captain was supreme on his quarterdeck. He had the power to enforce his orders at pistol point and punish offenders with the cat-o'-nine-tails. When Kidd was faced with insubordination, he could have set the unruly elements ashore and shipped some good seamen at East Indian ports.

After weighing all available evidence, it appears that Kidd, recalling the lush days of piracy in the Caribbean and his own experiences there, felt confident that he could bluff his way and establish his innocence, once he returned to the Atlantic coast. He set great store by the King's commission. He also felt confident that Bellomont and the great lords involved in the venture would protect him as they promised, if for no other reason than to safeguard their share of the loot.

He was further lulled into this sense of security by letters which had been sent to him in Madagascar by Livingston, and his friend James Emmot. They had already heard rumors that Kidd was not conducting himself with perfect legality in the Red Sea area. Both letters seem an attempt to reassure Kidd that he had nothing to fear when he got home.

Wrote Livingston: "You have not wanted [lacked] enemies who have endeavoured to give my Lord [Bellomont] bad impressions of you, but have been without any Effect." He went on to say that Bellomont had made many kind expressions in regard to Kidd, that he was "hearty in your Service . . . so that ye best returne ye can make . . . is to use your utmost Endeavours to Promote his and the rest of yr. owners' Intrest . . . by making a Speedy returne unto this place, where you may be assured to meet with a hearty welcome, and a friendship to support you against all ye mischances of yr. Voyage."

Kidd's friend Emmot wrote in the same vein. He had been talking to Bellomont about certain "flying reports" about Kidd: "His Lordship assured me there was no such thing, but on the contrary, he ever had a good opinion of Captain Kidd . . . I write, lest these false reports . . . if by any inadvertency, any necessity, or Insolency of yor. men you have made any false steps, if you come directly hence, which is my earnest advice to you, lett this assure you that there will be effectual care taken to limitt ye same."[2]

Emmot was plainly worried. Although Bellomont blandly assured Emmot of his faith in Kidd, the Earl secretly had a quite different view. He was convinced that Kidd had turned pirate. He had official advices from London to that effect. At the same time he was smart enough to realize that if he came out strongly and accused Kidd, he would never be able to catch him. The seas were broad and hiding places many. Unless Kidd could be induced to come home with his booty, he could never be tried for piracy and the backers of the enterprise would be in the very same boat as the rascally Fletcher.

So he wrote a friendly letter to Kidd, sending it also to Madagascar, referring to his staying abroad longer than expected, announcing the Earl's arrival in New York and referring to his talk with Kidd's friend Emmot, who "acquaints me that it would be gratefull to your wife and family to make this place the port of your Returne . . .

"I have consented to it, and desire that you will use your best Endeavours to hasten hither, where you shall meet with all ye Incouragements in my power to give you, and yt, you may not be discourage'd by the false Reports of ill men, you may be assured of haueing my Interest Employ'd to doe you all ye service you can reasonably desire with his Majesty, and ye rest of ye owners, and herein you may faithfully rely . . ."

Bellomont had no intention whatsoever of living up to this promise, as will soon be seen.

One of William Kidd's inherent traits was deceitfulness. This is brought out by what happened after he captured a Moorish ship soon after he turned pirate. The master of the vessel was a Dutchman and they had hoisted French colors after Kidd had chased the ship also under French colors. It will be recalled that Kidd had been given a letter of marque to prey on French shipping as an English privateer. After Kidd had satisfied himself that the commander of the vessel was a Dutchman, he noticed that a Frenchman was on board as a passenger. Kidd demanded whether the Frenchman had a pass for himself. The Frenchman said that he had. Realizing that this would be a good excuse for capturing the vessel he told the Frenchman that he must pretend to be the captain and "By God," said he, "you *are* the captain." This meant that Kidd was at liberty to seize the vessel as a legitimate French prize since her commander was French. This obvious subterfuge was to backlash on Kidd later on. Meanwhile Kidd sold the cargo and continued cruising. Once, having sighted a Dutch ship, his men were all for attacking her. Kidd opposed it. There was talk of mutiny and many of the crew wanted to get into the small boats and attack. Kidd told them angrily that if they did so he would never let them return on board. This was a rare occasion when Kidd stood up to his men and refused their demands.

In actual fact the vessel which Kidd's crew wished to attack was not Dutch at all. It was the *Loyall Captain*, belonging to a New York man named Captain Hoare. He was supposed to be a privateer, but was actually a pirate. Since Hoare's name was not on the list of the most wanted pirates, Kidd probably knew him and did not wish to attack.

His decision was badly received by his crew. As always, their ringleader was William Moore, the gunner. Moore had been ill with cholera, but was recovering. Yet all the while he was grumbling and bickering and encouraging the men to oppose the captain. One day as Kidd was walking along the deck he came upon Moore sharpening a chisel. The gunner was seething with resentment. As Kidd came up to him Moore cried, "You have brought us to ruin and we are desolate. I could have put you in the way of taking that ship and be none the worse for it." This was too much for Kidd. In a paroxysm of rage he picked up a wooden bucket and brought it down heavily on Moore's head. It must have cracked his skull, for he was dead within a day. Some said that Moore died of illness rather than from the blow. In any case the incident was to weigh heavily against Kidd at his trial.

Not long after Moore's death, Kidd's big chance hove in sight. It was a great vessel of four hundred tons belonging to a group of Armenian merchants. Her name was *Quedagh Merchant*. Kidd could tell by her rig that she was a local vessel and figured she could be easily taken. He chased her under French colors, threw a shot across her bow and ordered her to heave to, which she promptly did. Kidd sent a boat on board and discovered that the captain was an Englishman named Wright. This was not surprising, since the East Indians were not good navigators and often hired Dutchmen or Englishmen to command their vessels. Kidd made Wright prisoner along with two Dutchmen and a Frenchman. All the rest of the passengers and crew were Indians or Armenians.

The *Quedagh Merchant* carried one of the richest cargoes ever taken by the Red Sea Men, rivaled only by Captain Avery and his magnificent booty of diamonds. She carried an immense number of bales of rich fabrics, including bolts of silks and muslins embroidered in silver and gold; gold dust; gold in bars; gold coins; silver ingots; silver coins; pearls; coral beads; ivory; spices; sandalwood; rich clothing for men and women; hand-wrought jewelry and many other valuable items. The immense quantity of stuff awed even the most hardened looters of Kidd's crew.

The captain and officers of the *Quedagh Merchant* implored Kidd to release the ship and cargo upon the payment of a large ransom. The Armenians and Indians, no mean bargainers, offered twenty thousand rupees, which was about the equivalent of three thousand English pounds sterling. Kidd scoffed at this offer and decided that he would gain far more by selling off the cargo. He set the passengers and crew ashore at various points along the coast and trafficked with merchants in that part of the Indian Ocean.

Gradually over a period of weeks he disposed of part of the large cargo.

Kidd's deceitfulness is further shown by his treatment of the Indian merchants who came on board to buy the merchandise taken from the *Quedagh Merchant*. Captain Charles Johnson records in his book that as Kidd was about to sail, he decided to cheat them. "So he made no scruple about taking their goods and setting them on shore without any payment in money or goods, which they little expected, for as they had been used to dealing with pirates, they always found them men of honor in the way of trade, enemies to deceit and a people that scorned to rob but in their own way." Kidd was one of the exceptions.

When Kidd was ready to leave that part of the Indian Ocean, he put a prize crew aboard the *Quedagh Merchant* and in company with the *Adventure Galley*, headed for St. Mary. On arriving there, the *Adventure Galley* was so unseaworthy that she sank in the harbor. Kidd just barely had time to transfer aboard the *Quedagh Merchant*, which he renamed the *Adventure Prize*. Kidd never publicly admitted that the *Quedagh Merchant* and the *Adventure Prize* were one and the same ship. Why? Possibly to confuse his accusers.

Lying at St. Mary were a number of pirate vessels. They promptly sent small boats aboard Kidd to find out who he was. They did not know at this time that he was supposed to be out hunting for them. A number of the captains were old Caribbean hands who welcomed Kidd as a brother. Apparently the news had reached these pirates that Kidd was after them. Grinning, they told him that it would not be "very kind" of him to capture and hang them, since they had been pals together in the Caribbean. According to Johnson, "Kidd soon dissipated their doubts by swearing he had no such design, and that he was now in every respect their brother, and just as bad as they, and calling for a cup of Bomboo [a punch] drank their Captains' health." One of Kidd's old friends was none other than the notorious Captain Culliford, the very same man who had stolen a vessel from Kidd years before in the Caribbean. Culliford had had good luck and was now commander of a pirate vessel named the *Resolution*, a native vessel once known as the *Mocco* or *Mocha Merchant*. In spite of Culliford's theft, Kidd got on pleasant terms with him, and went aboard his ship. He assured Culliford of his dedication as a pirate and even presented him with an anchor and some guns so that Culliford could go back roving.

Since Kidd had already divided among his crew, as agreed, most of the gold, silver and gems taken so far, he now sold off some more merchandise and divided the proceeds. Although Kidd was honest with his crew in the division of the loot, they still felt resentment against him, for they plundered his sea chest and stole his papers including the log, which, according to his Commission from the King, he was required to keep and in which he was to set down all of his actions, day by day. Some of the men even threatened his life and several times Kidd had to lock himself in the cabin to prevent his being murdered. Nor was he astonished when many of his men deserted him and signed on with Culliford.

Now Kidd found himself with only forty hands to sail the *Adventure Prize* back to America, for he had decided that he had had enough. On the way home the vessel touched at Amboyna, one of the Dutch Spice Islands. Here Kidd received news that he had been posted as a pirate.

At last Kidd's actions had begun to catch up with him. His plundering of the coast, his cheating of Indian merchants, his imprisonment of his fellow countrymen, and his piratical captures had created a storm of indignation among the stockholders of the English East India Company as well as among members of Parliament. A number of motions in Parliament were made to investigate Kidd, his Commission, and the man who sent him out, Lord Bellomont. The unfortunate Earl had placed himself in a dangerous political position not only because of his choice of Kidd as a pirate chaser, but also because he was part of the syndicate which had put up the money to fit out Kidd's ship. Since this syndicate was composed of high-ranking government officials, the jaundiced eye of suspicion was cast on this Whig group by their political opponents the Tories, who accused them of outfitting a pirate rather than a pirate chaser.

Because another wave of antipirate feeling was sweeping England, Parliament thought the easiest solution to the problem would be to publish a proclamation offering the King's Free Pardon to all pirates who would voluntarily surrender themselves regardless of the piracies they had committed. They were given until the last day of April 1699 to submit. The King's Pardon was restricted to those pirates who operated eastward from the Cape of Good Hope. Captains Avery and Kidd and several others were specifically excluded from the King's Pardon.

Kidd was unaware of this proclamation at the time he left Amboyna en route to the Atlantic coast. He was not too much concerned with his own situation, since he relied heavily upon Lord Bellomont and his friends. He also had as an alibi two French passes which he had taken from ships he had captured. He convinced himself that these would put a good face on the matter and refute the charge of piracy.

Another factor that may have added to Kidd's optimism was the easygoing treatment accorded to pirates by previous governors of the American colonies, particularly Fletcher. No doubt Kidd thought that if Bellomont received a handsome return on his investment he would shrug the whole matter off. Kidd badly misjudged his sponsor.

We next find Kidd anchoring the *Adventure Prize* in the shelter of the small West Indian island of Anguilla, in April 1699. Here again he had news of his own misdoings, together with the Proclamation of Pardon for all Red Sea Men except himself, Avery, and a few others.

At St. Mary, Kidd had taken on as passengers a number of pirates who wanted to go home. Some worked their way. Others paid the usual hundred dollar fee. There was much discussion and some anxious looks when these pirate passengers heard about the King's offer of pardon and Kidd's indictment for piracy. To make matters worse, it was said that a British squadron was hunting for Kidd. Rear Admiral Benbow and the colonial governors of the various provinces had received a circular from Parliament stating that the Lords Justices, having received information about "the notorious piracies committed by Captain Kidd and of his having seized and plundered diverse ships, their Excellencies had given orders to the commander of the squadron fitted down for the East Indies . . . to pursue and seize said Kidd . . . and his accomplices."

The circular also stated that the victims of robberies committed by Kidd were to be compensated and that Kidd was to be prosecuted "with the utmost vigour of the law."

From Anguilla, Kidd sailed to the island of St. Thomas in the Danish West Indies. Here he asked the Governor for permission to take on provisions for the voyage north. But the Danish Governor had already heard of Kidd's piracy and refused either to allow him to buy stores or even to anchor in the harbor. Nevertheless the pirates went ashore to trade, carouse and spend their money. A slightly different version of Kidd's encounter with the Danish Governor of St. Thomas is contained in the MS diary of Narcissus Luttrell, a London lawyer, preserved in the Library of All Souls, Oxford:

"August 17, 1699. Letters from Curassau [Curaçao, Dutch West Indies] say that the famous pyrat Captain Kidd, in a ship of 30 guns and 250 men, offered the Danish governor of St. Thomas 45,000 peices of eight in gold and a great present in gold, if he would protect him a month, which he refused . . ."

This would indicate that Kidd might well have had the idea of delaying his return to America, hoping the agitation against him would subside. Or he might even have considered not returning home at all, taking refuge in the Danish West Indies, out of the reach of British law.

Père Labat, a Catholic missionary-priest, visited St. Thomas some time afterwards and recorded Kidd's stay in his memoirs[3] as follows: "Some two years ago a great pirate ship, manned by a crew of all nations but chiefly by Englishmen, was run ashore at St. Thomas by her crew, who then slipped away, one by one, as no country would receive them in a body. These pirates had pillaged the ships of the Great Mogul laden with women, merchandise and enormous treasure for Mexico,[4] and they had loaded their great ship with an incredible quantity of the richest Indian silks and muslins. People who had traded with the pirates when they were still on their ship bought these stuffs very cheaply, an *aune* of muslin embroidered with gold could be obtained for only 20 sols and the rest of the cargo in proportion. The pirates had circulated through the Islands great quantities of precious stones and gold coins of Asia, which we call sequins . . . Arabian characters were inscribed on both sides of these coins . . .

"Many merchants of St. Thomas had filled their stores with these Indian stuffs, and sold them at a cheaper rate than the merchants of Martinique . . ." where Labat had his headquarters.

The shrewd priest himself did not ignore these bargains, for he records: "I used all the money I had and 200 écus more that I borrowed, to buy as much of these materials as I could, not only for ourselves, but for our friends who, I felt sure, would be pleased to have them."

Labat's statement that Kidd ran the *Adventure Prize* ashore at St. Thomas is incorrect, for it was based only on hearsay. The fact is that the vessel was sailed to a remote spot on the southeast coast of Hispaniola, remained there for some time and months later was set afire. There still remained a good deal of merchandise aboard, mostly fabrics. No doubt Kidd figured that if he brought this great ship to New York or Boston, it would be tangible proof that he had turned pirate. So he placed the vessel and its contents in charge of Henry Bolton, a former Collector of Customs of the British Island of Antigua, who was now a merchant with a lively trade throughout the Caribbean.

Bolton sold Kidd a seaworthy sloop named the *Antonio* for the voyage north. Kidd selected choice bales of merchandise from the *Adventure Prize* and loaded them aboard the *Antonio*, along with his many chests containing the gold, silver, precious gems and ornaments he had stolen from the ships he had captured. Then, with the remnant of his crew and passengers, he headed for home.

But before he hoisted sail, he did one more thing that gave him a great deal of satisfaction: he set ashore his troublesome, grumbling brother-in-law, Samuel Bradley, on a desolate point of land with only his sea chest for company, although Bradley was quite ill. All along Bradley had upbraided Kidd for his actions and kept urging him to give himself up. No doubt Kidd hoped he would die at St. Thomas. In this he was disappointed, for Bradley survived, made his way to Carolina, and signed a deposition against Kidd.

On the way north, some of Kidd's men began to get worried. They knew full well that their captain had been posted as a pirate. To be seen with him was virtually an indictment of themselves. So when the *Antonio* arrived at the mouth of Delaware Bay a number of Kidd's men went ashore in small boats intending to disappear quietly among the towns and country districts of Jersey and other provinces. They landed in Cape May. Although they did not know it at the time, they had been preceded by another group of pirates who had come ashore at the same place from Captain Giles Shelley's vessel the *Nassau*. Shelley, the very same man who was Livingston's friend and confidant, was now a notorious pirate-trader.

In heaving to off Cape May, Kidd was violating his commission, for he had been told to return directly from the Red Sea without touching at any American port before reaching New York or Boston.

Once ashore, Kidd's men scattered. They passed themselves off as honest merchant seamen or privateersmen. But the strange Arabic coins they tossed about quickly stamped these rascals as Red Sea Men. Soon there was a great hue and cry to run them down, seize their loot and put them in jail.

These men had good reason to be apprehensive. They knew that even if they submitted to the King's Pardon, they might be refused and tried and found guilty of piracy. Some of their own shipmates had had this experience. Others who did not fear the noose were loath to settle down to honest pursuits. They were still dreaming of their happy days in the Red Sea and intended to return as soon as possible.

After weighing anchor off Cape May, Kidd pursued a cautious and devious course of action. From Cape May he wrote a letter announcing his return to Bellomont. It was carried to Boston where the Earl was staying. This letter has never beeen found, but apparently it was to sound out Bellomont's temper. In any case, Kidd judged it best not to put into New York although he knew his wife would be waiting for him there. Instead, he sailed in June 1699 along the south shore of Long Island, rounded Montauk Point and anchored off Gardiner's Island. This spot of land is located about midway between Orient Point and Montauk Point in Gardiner's Bay, with Block Island Sound to the east. Approximately four miles long, the island was a land grant to the Gardiner family by the king of England. John (Lord) Gardiner was the third generation to live there and was in residence when Kidd anchored a half mile offshore.

Curious about the strange ship, Gardiner was rowed out to the sloop by his servants. He was greeted politely by Captain Kidd, who lost no time in asking (or rather demanding) the help of Gardiner. The proprietor of Gardiner's Island, surrounded by murderous-looking men, knew better than to refuse. He had had several rough experiences with privateersmen (Kidd pretended to be one) and knew that if he did not comply it would go hard with him. Kidd's first request was to take three Negro slaves ashore. Some time later Kidd landed two bales of merchandise and another Negro in exchange for which he demanded six sheep and a barrel of cider. As a present for Gardiner's wife, Kidd sent some muslin which had been damaged by sea water.

Gardiner's servants who helped Kidd's men in landing the merchandise were paid in Arabian gold.

After three days Kidd left Gardiner's Island and stood

off Block Island. Meanwhile he had sent one of his men named Clark to Gardiner with this message: "I want you to . . . keep for me to my order a chest and a box of gold, a bundle of quilts, four bailes of gold cloth. This box of gold is intended for Lord Bellomont." It was Gardiner himself who took charge of the loot together with two thirty-pound bags of silver coins. He gave a receipt for them to Kidd's man. As a present for Gardiner himself, there were a sash, a pair of worsted stockings and some gold and gold dust weighing about a pound. Later this gift was followed by a barrel of sugar.

All this while Gardiner claimed he did not know that Kidd was a pirate. If he suspected, he said nothing. It is quite likely that Gardiner was telling the truth, for he made a deposition before a justice of the peace in Boston a little later, describing his meetings with Kidd and claiming that he knew nothing of his dubious character.

Many stories and legends stem from Kidd's visit to Gardiner's Island. Most of them deal with buried treasure and are figments of the imagination. It is true, however, that Kidd *did* leave a chest with Lord Gardiner. But it did not contain the fifty pounds of gold which Robert Livingston later claimed Kidd had buried on the island. On the contrary, the chest contained, according to Kidd's own deposition, flowered silks, muslins, calico, gold cloth, silk striped with silver and gold, a bushel of cloves and nutmegs and some semi-precious stones. All of it, Kidd declared, had been "bought" at Madagascar.

It has been well established that during the days that Kidd was anchored off Block Island (where his wife and children visited him) he secretly sent a large part of his treasure to various friends for safekeeping. At the same time, Kidd wrote another letter to the Earl of Bellomont through his friend James Emmot. This man was a prominent admiralty lawyer of New York. He had a shady reputation and was hated by Bellomont.

It is not hard to imagine the state of mind of the Earl, from the moment Kidd had been posted as a pirate until he returned home. All this time Bellomont had been seething with rage. His own position was not only embarrassing, it was dangerous. He had sponsored, in all good faith, a supposedly honest merchant captain and privateersman to track down and capture notorious pirates in the Red Sea. He was also the principal financier of the expedition, acting on behalf of himself and four high Whig officials. Yet the man in whom he had the utmost faith turned out to be a common high seas robber who came back loaded with illicit booty, blandly declaring his innocence.

Bellomont was lying in wait for him and had already baited the trap. Months before, realizing that the only thing to be done was to clap Kidd in jail the moment he set foot ashore, Bellomont had received orders to this effect from Secretary of State James Vernon in Whitehall.

Meanwhile, out on the placid waters near Block Island, Kidd was receiving visitors aboard the *Antonio*. One was Duncan Campbell, a bookseller and postmaster of Boston. When Kidd's wife and children left the sloop they carried with them a handsome amount of loot. It was also known that Kidd sent two sloops into New York with merchandise.

Now Bellomont was ready to act. He wrote Kidd a wheedling letter, saying that if the captain could demonstrate his innocence, Lord Bellomont would "undertake to get him a King's Pardon."

This was exactly what Kidd was fishing for. All along he had been creating for himself an image of innocence. When he had read the Earl's letter, he happily went ashore in Boston to the handsome home of his friend Duncan Campbell. A few hours later he was seized by a constable. Kidd half drew his sword but was quickly disarmed and clapped in jail.

All along Kidd had been counting on those French passes to give him a clean bill of health. But to his consternation when they were shown to Bellomont, the Earl took the passes and kept them. They never appeared at Kidd's trial. Bellomont had good reason to withhold them. He wanted Kidd found guilty and hanged as promptly as possible. But if those passes had been placed in evidence in London at the trial, they would at least have partly vindicated the charge of piracy against Kidd and prolonged the whole miserable affair. It was not until 1920 that the French passes were discovered in the Public Records Office in London by author Ralph Paine.

In 1699 there was no English law which authorized trials for piracy in the American colonies. The accused had to be sent to England. Since communications between provincial officials and the Crown depended on slow sailing ships, it took months before Bellomont received the necessary clearance from London for Kidd to be shipped to England, along with a number of other men charged with piracy. By now it was March 1700. A total of nine months elapsed between the time Kidd was put in irons and the day he was sent aboard the frigate *Advice*, bound for England.

Meanwhile Kidd had not been idle. From jail he wrote long letters to the Lords of the Admiralty, stating his case and declaring himself innocent. Yet his confidence was slowly seeping away. His friends, to whom he had entrusted much of his loot, ignored him. Now aboard an English man-of-war, he had little to look forward to except a stormy voyage, another long wait in jail, and a trial that could well terminate his career at the end of a rope.

Bellomont's parting remark about the prisoner was far from complimentary: "There never was a greater Lyar or Thief in the World, than this Kidd."

It was on a gallows such as this that Captain Kidd was hanged at Wapping, near London, May 23, 1701. (From an old print.)

10

William Kidd,
Gallows Bait

KIDD's confinement in the Boston jail had told on his health. He had been kept under close guard and in irons most of the time. On the voyage to England he became ill and made a feeble attempt at suicide by a few slashes on his wrist.

After a stormy voyage of fifty-three days, the *Advice* came to anchor in the Thames and Kidd was lodged in Newgate Prison. Some of the men who had gone ashore at Cape May from the *Antonio* and others who had remained with Kidd were lodged in the same prison. They were Nicholas Churchill, Hugh Parrot, Richard Barlicorn, Abel Owens, and Darby Mullins. Some of them claimed to have surrendered to Governor Bass of West Jersey and submitted to the King's Pardon within the time limit. They were confident that they would be set free. Kidd had no such prospect, for he had been specifically excluded by name in the proclamation.

By the time Kidd reached London he had become the focal point of a bitter political feud between Whigs and Tories. The ironic part of Kidd's situation was that even if he had remained honest he would have been scorned by provincial and English merchants who were making fortunes in stolen merchandise. If he had swept piracy from the Red Sea, he would have been the most unpopular man in America and in danger of being ruined financially.

So now we see Kidd, languishing in prison, charged with murder and piracy and bound to lose one way or another. If he is acquitted, his name will be anathema in his home town and he will never be able to re-establish himself with the wealthy and aristocratic crooks who rule the roost. If he is convicted, he will be hoisted high on the gallows.

In addition to being a political football, Kidd, thanks to extraordinary publicity, had become a bloody villain and "arch pyrate" in the minds of the public. No one came to his aid. The people of England and Scotland despised him for a man who had been sent out to chase pirates and had become one himself.

Meanwhile the Tories saw a ripe opportunity to wreak political havoc on the Whigs. They promptly started impeachment proceedings against four Whig aristocrats: the Earl of Portland, Lord Somers, the Earl of Orford, and Lord Halifax. Lord Somers and the Earl of Orford had been secret members of the syndicate which financed Kidd's expedition.

Somers had already been in trouble and had been forced from the Chancellorship. Now the Tories tied him directly with Captain Kidd. They declared that he had abused his position as Lord High Chancellor by placing the Great Seal of England on Kidd's commission. Although Lord Halifax was not connected with the Kidd affair, he was also a target for the Tories and was forced to resign as Chancellor of the Exchequer.

The whole situation played directly into the hands of the Tories. Kidd was the chief villain. Like shrewd politicians, they thumped the drum and blew the bugle until the Kidd case became a *cause célèbre* throughout the British Isles.

The Tories purposely delayed the trial of Kidd to prolong their campaign against the Whigs. Even though Parliament was in session at the time of Kidd's arrival, it was not until March 27 and 31, 1701, that Kidd was examined by the House of Commons. Promptly the next day impeachment messages against Kidd's aristocratic backers were sent to the House of Lords.

Nothing much resulted from Kidd's examination. "He confessed nothing material." Lord Halifax, in an effort to set matters straight, visited Kidd secretly at Newgate Prison, but when this became known there was a great outcry and the keeper of the prison was removed.

Early in May, things speeded up. The impeachment proceedings and the trial for piracy began almost simultaneously. The accusations against the Earl of Portland contained ten articles, two of which involved him with Kidd. Lord Somers was cited in fourteen articles, one of which specifically mentioned Kidd.

Now began the lengthy business of recording the testimony of witnesses for and against Captain Kidd at his trial at Old Bailey. Among them was Kidd's "doctor," Bradenham, who was described at the time as a "desperate pyratical villain" and "a blade of fortune." One interesting bit of information brought out by Bradenham was that when the *Adventure Galley* touched at the Cape Verde Islands, provisions ran so short that several of the sailors had to sell their clothes to the natives and use the money to buy food. It is

doubtful whether this was the actual truth. It is more probable that the provisions aboard the *Adventure Galley* were
so poor and limited that when the men went ashore they
sold some of their personal effects to get a square meal.

When Kidd's ship lay off Bab's Key waiting for a fleet of
Indian ships, Bradenham swore that Kidd remarked that he
would "take as many of them as he could, for he intended
if possible to ballast his ship with Silver and Gold." But
Kidd's design was thwarted by a heavily armed frigate
which "made Kidd shear off and leave that designe."

Turning to attack another ship, commanded by an Englishman, Parker, Bradenham claimed that Kidd "did order
some of his men to tye some of the moores [Moors] their
hands behind them and hoist ym. up by a takle and to Drub
them on the back with a cutlace [cutlass] . . . but there was
no treasure on board and soe he left her to ye moores that
were on board her."

Bradenham's testimony also described the capture of the
Quedagh Merchant: he told how Kidd had chased her under
French colors and she also had put out French colors. An
old Frenchman identified himself as captain of the ship, but
later admitted that Wright,[1] an Englishman, was the actual
master. Kidd told his own crew that the Frenchman had
shown him French passes which gave him authority to capture the *Quedagh Merchant* as an enemy ship. However,
Bradenham did not state that anyone actually saw these
documents.

On returning from his greatest haul, Kidd was actually
piloted into St. Mary's harbor by the notorious pirate Culliford, Bradenham declared. The money and gold taken from
the *Quedagh Merchant* had been shared out on the coast of
Malabar. Upon arrival at St. Mary, according to Bradenham, a division was made of part of the valuable merchandise from the hold of the *Quedagh Merchant*. Each man

received a share to the value of two hundred pieces of eight.

Bradenham's testimony continued: "Sometime after the death of gunner Moore . . . Captain Kidd said: 'I do not care so much for the death of my gunner . . . for I have good friends that will bring me off of that. . .' " Bradenham also claimed that before Moore's murder, he was not aware of any altercations or enmity between Kidd and his gunner.

Other witnesses added to the pile of incriminating evidence against Kidd.

Joseph Palmer of Westchester County, New York, a member of Kidd's crew, described Kidd's attack on Moore. He stated that Kidd took up a bucket to which was attached a leather strap. Kidd whirled it around his head and let it fly at Moore while the gunner was bringing a "chissel on deck." After the injured Moore was taken below to the gun room he said to his mates, "Captain Kidd has given me his last blow."

Then Kidd was reported to have shouted down the stairs, "You are a villain! Damn you!"

Moore died the next day.

Palmer further testified that when Kidd met the pirate Culliford at Madagascar he was overheard to tell him: "It is not true I have come to take you . . . I am as bad as you are." He promised not to interfere with Culliford's piratical activities. It was also said that Kidd shared a bowl of punch with him and gave him a handsome brace of pistols.

Bradenham's testimony, while partly true, is open to grave suspicion on the grounds of exaggeration and personal enmity toward Kidd. Kidd was bitter against Bradenham for his testimony. On the last day of his trial, Kidd declared, "This man tells a thousand lies . . . you are a Rogue."[2]

In attempting to refute Palmer's evidence about capturing English ships and declaring them to be French, Kidd blamed his crew for forcing him to make the capture. "I would have given these ships to them again, but you would not, you all voted against it . . . Did I not ask you where will you carry the ship *Quedagh Merchant* and you said we will make a prize of her and we will carry her to Madagascar?"

It is surprising that the commander of a ship carrying a commission from King William would submit to a vote of his crew! This was a common practice among pirates, but certainly not aboard a privateer carrying an official letter of marque.

In supplying further evidence, Palmer gives an interesting description of how Captain Kidd shared out the prize money after the capture of the *Quedagh Merchant*.

"When Captain Kidd shared the money . . . he called every Man by the List and they came in with their Hats in the Hands, and he gave them their money in the Great Cabin, and they sloughed it up in their hats and went away."

Robert Bradenham, Joseph Palmer, and Theophilus Turner, each of whom was also accused of piracy, fared far better than Kidd. Because as witnesses they supplied sworn testimony against their captain, they were pardoned. Part of the wording of the pardon is interesting:

Because they were "made use off as witnesses . . . we are graciously pleased in consideration of the promises to extend our grace and mercy unto them, and have hereby thought fitt to signifye our will and pleasure to you that you cause them . . . to be inserted in our first and most general pardon that shall come out for the poor convicts of Newgate, for all pyracies . . . any of them done and committed at any time before the day of the date thereof, and that in the meantime you take baile for their appearance in order to plead their said pardon, and for soe doing this shall be a warrant." This rare document was given at Hampton Court on May 26, 1701, by the command of King William.

When Kidd was given an opportunity to speak, he gave this story of his conflict with Gunner Moore to Lord Chief Justice Ward. It did Kidd little good in the eyes of His Lordship, but it is interesting to record it verbatim:

"My Lord, I will tell you what the case was: I was coming within a League of the Dutchman, and some of my Men were making a mutiny about taking her; and my Gunner told the People he could put the Captain in a way to take the ship and be safe. Says I, 'How will you do that?' The Gunner answered, 'We will take the captain and Men aboard.' 'And what then?' 'We will go aboard the ship and plunder her, and we will have it under their hands [in their writing] that we did not take her.' Says I, 'May we take this Ship because we are Poor?' Upon that a mutiny arose, so I took up a Bucket and just throwed it at him and said, 'You are a Rogue to make such a Motion.' That I can prove, my Lord."

It is very likely that Kidd was telling the truth, when he cried to Judge Ward, in regard to Moore's murder, "It was not designedly done, but in my passion, for which I am heartily sorry."

Kidd's trial flushed out another Red Sea Man, the notorious Captain Giles Shelley, of whom we have heard before. He was hiding in London, trying to avoid publicity. It was this man, a crony of Livingston's, who made a fortune by taking a floating arsenal from New York to the pirates in Madagascar, who were short of guns and ammunition. Shelley was about to decamp aboard a brigantine to get out of the limelight. Some said he was bound for the Red Sea. Others said the West Indies. In any case, he was dragged before the authorities and gave unwilling testimony. It was probably more to save his own hide than anything else. He declared that Kidd was not looked upon as a pirate but as one who sailed under the King's commission. He also swore that he did not see Kidd in Madagascar during the whole time that Kidd was there. He ended by saying, "Kidd lives at New Yorke, when at home, and is my neighbor. I have not seen Kidd since I went to Madagascar, nor since my returne till I saw him about two months ago at Newgate." Did Kidd tell Shelley to be as noncommittal as possible and not reveal what went on far away in Madagascar? It is possible, since Shelley admitted he had seen Kidd at Newgate.

Now it might seem that Kidd, realizing that everything was going against him, would turn against the distinguished backers of his expedition. Certainly he was aware of the implications of his trial and could have made things very embarrassing for the men who had greedily hoped to profit by exterminating the Red Sea Men. But not a word came from Kidd's lips. One could hardly blame him if it had.

A story circulated at this time was that when a man named Kisdale was drinking coffee with Kidd at Newgate Prison (the captain was allowed certain liberties) Kisdale said to Kidd: "You are a fool to be hang'd for anybody, and you may certainly save your life if you will speak against the Lord Orford and the Lord Somers." Kidd replied: "I will hang for nobody and am resolved to speak all I know."[3]

The key words here are "all I know." It should be recalled that at no time did the names of these noble Lords appear on any documents connected with Kidd. Although the public well knew that they were backers of his expedition, it would have been very difficult to prove so in a court of law from documentary evidence. Also it is very unlikely that any of the principals in this expedition would tell on each other. For example, it is highly unthinkable that Lord Bellomont or Robert Livingston would have given evidence against their titled, secret partners.

By this time Kidd was in a wretched physical and mental state. He had been severely treated from the time he landed in England. For a while he was kept in irons. At all times he was kept in close confinement except at certain hours of the day. He had to appeal to the authorities to permit him to see his relatives, obtain clean clothes and medical attention. Finally the authorities relented sufficiently to allow him to take a certain amount of exercise in the prison yard and to have a drink now and then with approved visitors at the "ordinary" in the prison.

But even more unfortunately for Kidd, he had been deprived of all of his papers, which had been seized when he was taken into custody. The most important of these were the French passes upon which he relied to prove his innocence of the charge of piracy. It will be recalled that these had been taken from him by Lord Bellomont, and Kidd had not seen them since. He kept up a stream of letters to various authorities, trying to secure all his papers so as to prepare some sort of defense.

No one stepped forward to defend this man. In similar circumstances today, a trial lawyer, appointed by the court, would appear to take Kidd's case. But Captain William Kidd then had no one. The reason? This was a political situation as well as a court trial and no lawyer would dare fly in the face of the Tories who had so successfully sharpened their axes against the Whigs.

Here is an excerpt from Kidd's letter to Robert Harley, Speaker of the House of Commons. It was written from Newgate Jail about April 1701:

> May it please Y'r. Honour,
> I hope I have not offended against Law, but if I have, It was the fault of others who knew better and made me the Tool of their Ambition and Avarice, and who may perhaps think it in their Interest that I should be removed out of the world.
> I did not seek the commission I undertook, but was partly

Cajold and partly menac'd into it by the Lord Bellomont and one Robert Livingston of New York, projector and promoter and Chief Manager of the design, and he only can give the House a satisfactory account of all the transactions of my owners. He was the man admitted into their Closet and received their private instructions which he kept in his own hands, and he encouraged me in their names to doe more than I ever did and to act without regard to my Commission! I was in great Consternation when I was before that Great Assembly, Your Honourable House, which, with the disadvantage of a mean Capacity, want of Education, and a Spirit cramp't by Long Confinement, made me uncapable of representing my Case . . .

I humbly beg your Compassion and Protection of the Hon'ble the House of Commons, and yo'r Honour's intercession with them in behalfe of

Y'r Honour's Most Dutifull and Distress'd Servant,

Wm. Kidd.

Truly a pitiable letter. Much of what Kidd wrote was true. He points the accusing finger at Livingston, who undoubtedly was, as Kidd declares, the evil "projector and promoter and Chief Manager of the design." This letter almost cries out in despair, for it reveals Kidd's inability to defend himself in court and his strong feeling of inferiority. Members of his own crew had put up a better defense in court than he had.

Kidd's letter went on to reiterate his claim that he was not guilty of the crime of piracy charged against him and accused Bellomont of withholding his precious French passes and other documents which Kidd believed would clear him. He had been told by the Council that "it will little avail me without producing the passes themselves."

Kidd was trapped and he knew it.

Some weeks after Kidd wrote that letter, the House of Commons agreed that he could have a copy of his commission and "such other papers as are necessary for him, to make his defense, and that the said copyes of the papers are to be given out by Mr. Joddrell . . ."

This Joddrell was an official of the High Court of Admiralty. It has been claimed that it was Joddrell, contrary to the orders of the House of Commons, who withheld many papers essential to Kidd's defense, including his French passes. It is unknown who ordered Joddrell to withhold this key evidence, but there is a suspicion that it was the judge of the high court or some other powerful officials close to the King himself.

More than a year had now elapsed since Kidd arrived in England. There had been delay after delay in holding his trial. Who was responsible? An accusing finger has been pointed to Sir Charles Hedges, a high church Tory who was Secretary of State. He had come in with the new Tory ministry in December 1700. At this time King William III was extremely unpopular with the English people. After giving Kidd a perfunctory examination shortly after his arrival, the Admiralty Board "sealed up the examinations to be preserved secret for the House of Commons . . . after the rising of the last Parliament." His Majesty, dining at the house of a noble lord, was heard to say, "If by the law of England he [the King] could be a witness, he could of his own knowledge justify the lords concern'd in all they had done in the affair of Kidd."[4]

When Kidd was indicted on charges of murder and piracy, he refused to plead one way or the other. He was told by the Recorder of the court, "Mr. Kidd, I must tell you, that if you will not plead you must have judgment against you as standing mute."

Whereupon Kidd mumbled, "Not guilty."

The most diligent research on Kidd's imprisonment and trial can lead to only one conclusion: the authorities were out to get him. Even if Kidd had been able to produce the French passes it seems almost certain that he would have been hanged for the murder of Moore, if for no other reason. Even though Kidd had written to the Earl of Romney and the Earl of Orford, they were successful in keeping out of the mess.

The finale of Kidd's trial is recorded in a diary of the day written by one Luttrell, as follows: "Thursday, 8 May, 1701. This afternoon Captain Kidd was found guilty of murder, for killing a seaman on board a ship, also of one piracy and tomorrow will be tryed upon for others.

"Saturday, 10 May 1701. Captain Kidd is found guilty upon six indictments of pyracy, and eight other pirates are condemn'd."

When asked by the clerk of Arraigns whether he had anything to say following his trial, Kidd replied hopelessly, "I will not trouble the court any more, for it is folly."

Why was Kidd found guilty of *murder* instead of simple manslaughter? All evidence points to the fact that Kidd hit Moore with a bucket in a blind fit of passion. It was not premeditated. Yet he was found guilty of first degree murder, which made hanging mandatory.

So now William Kidd must hang by the neck until he is dead and "May God have mercy on your soul." He must hang, not only because he is convicted of murder in the first degree, but also on several counts of piracy on the high seas; perhaps most important of all was the fact that he must hang to assure the Tories a political triumph over the Whigs.

It is a pity that no authentic portrait of William Kidd is known to exist. There have been one or two paintings which are alleged to be the man. It is surprising that no one made a painting or drawing or engraving of this notorious man, for his brief year of fame touched off a welter of broadsides, news sheets, poems and doggerel recounting his exploits. Kidd had captured the public fancy because, in its mind, he personified the "arch-pyrate" who combined in himself the bloody deeds of a generation of sea rovers. Iron-ically, he failed to measure up even to a pale copy of the picture so created. Kidd undoubtedly started life as an hon-est, seafaring man. But he was a poor disciplinarian, unable to control his crew of old buccaneers, was weak-willed in crises and worse still, flattered himself that he could bluff his way to freedom.

Kidd not only was destined to suffer the degradation of hanging, but he was also to receive the further disgrace of hanging in chains. This grisly practice was reserved only for the very worst criminals. Its purpose was to display the pitiful cadaver to public view and to warn other would-be sinners against the law to "look, mark well and mind your ways!"

On May 23, 1701, John Cheeke, gentleman Marshal of the Admiralty, received Kidd from the jailer at Newgate. Cheeke was instructed to take Kidd and several other con-demned pirates to the public gallows by the banks of the river Thames "above the flowing and ebbing of the tide-water . . . before the bank called Wapping, there lying and situated." He was further instructed to "suspend them by the neck, or cause them to be suspended until they or any of them be dead, according to the law of the sea and observed from time of old."[5]

The execution of pirates at this time was a gala occasion. It was an occasion for rejoicing, drinking, fights and rioting, all in good fun in honor of the due process of English law.

Promptly at the hour appointed, several tumbrils drew up in front of Newgate Prison. Soon a great crowd gathered, hooting and jeering as the condemned men were hustled into the open carts, standing glumly, securely handcuffed and with heavy shackles on their legs. Then the grim cor-tege began its slow progress toward Execution Dock. At this period it was traditional that the progress of condemned men toward the gallows was accompanied by a certain amount of ceremonial, intended to impress irresponsible men with the majesty of English law and the consequences of folly and evil.

It was three o'clock in the afternoon and the Marshal of the Admiralty led the procession, garbed in his robes of office. Immediately behind him marched the Deputy Marshal bearing the silver oar, symbol of the Admiralty and Probate Division of the law courts. On either side of the tumbrils marched the Marshal's men, heavily armed and keeping a watchful eye on the condemned.

Behind the procession came a mob of slum dwellers, whores, thieves, pickpockets and curious citizens, yelling huzzahs for the Admiralty Marshal and curses for the pirates. On rumbled the carts over the cobbles of Cheapside, past the Royal Exchange, all with great pomp. The procession traveled for another hour, passing the Tower of London, on through the slum area, which no doubt assailed the nostrils of the stately Marshal, for the place was full of rookeries, pigsties and vile dens. Here the crowd became thicker. The streets were jammed with a rag, tag and bobtail crowd of sailors, guttersnipes and frowsy harpies who shrieked, clamored, danced, and held up mugs of foaming ale in derision of the pirates. Many held out dirty hands, begging for a bit of Arabian gold or a gem or ring from men who would no longer need them.

At five o'clock the procession reached the foreshore, close to Wapping Old Stairs. Here stood the "grim waterish tree" (actually a gallows) commonly known as "Jack Ketch." The mob was now in full cry, shrieking and roaring, cracking coarse jokes, and hurling oaths at the pirates.

According to law, the time of the hanging was carefully calculated to take place at low tide.

To the Ordinary of Newgate (chaplain of the jail) named Paul Lorraine, the hanging of pirates offered a rare opportunity to turn the minds of evil men toward God, and secure statements and confessions of their sins before they were jerked into the devil's arms. This chaplain, an unctuous and hypocritical creature, also saw a golden chance to make money by recording and publishing the last hours of the criminals. This he promptly did and entitled it *The Only True Account of the Dying Speeches of the Condemn'd Pirates*. He knew that the public would eagerly pay a penny or two for an eyewitness report of the hanging and an account of the confessions of the pirates on the scaffold.

The shrewd chaplain also had a flair for advertising, for he placed a reading notice in a newspaper called the *Postboy*, telling about his forthcoming "only true account." He ended his advertisement with this warning: "Beware of Sham Papers, there being no true Account printed but this!"

Chaplain Lorraine's attempt to convert Kidd was unsuccessful. He admitted afterwards that "I found (to my unspeakable grief) when he [Kidd] was brought thither [to the place of hanging], he was enflamed with Drink, which had so discomposed his mind that it was in a very ill frame." But the stubborn clergyman did not give up. Soon a praying contest began between him and a rival clergyman. The two men stood at the foot of the gallows, exhorting, praying, shouting, straining to save the soul of William Kidd. All that Kidd muttered was that all masters of ships and mariners should be warned to have a care of themselves not to follow in his footsteps.

Lorraine's efforts had a better effect on Darby Mullins, a young member of Kidd's crew. He gratified Lorraine by declaring that all young men, "but especially Saylors, to take timely warning to avoid covetousness and all vain and idle company, lest ruin and misery overtook them before they were aware."

As Lorraine sang a penitential song, Darby Mullins and a French pirate loudly invoked God and Christ for mercy.

At last the religious part of the show came to an end and

it was time to hang Kidd. Even at the very end, the unfortunate captain's luck deserted him. After the noose had been adjusted around his neck and the trap sprung, Kidd's weight broke the rope and he fell heavily to the ground. Still alive but purple in the face and speechless, he was hanged a second time. The rope held and Kidd sailed into eternity.

The frenzied chaplain looked upon this incident as a fortunate chance for more exhortation: "For the last time I prayed with him with a greater satisfaction than I had before that he was penitent." There is reason to believe that the chaplain was stretching the truth to the breaking point merely to picture himself as having triumphed over Kidd and the devil at the last moment. It is questionable how a man half strangled could possibly be penitent.

The pirates Churchill, Howe, Loffe, Hugh Parrot, Able Owen, Robert Hickman and John Eldridge were reprieved at the last moment.

Kidd remained hanging from the gallows until three full tides had ebbed and flowed, according to law. Afterwards, his corpse was subjected to the fate reserved only for the most notorious criminals.

The process of hanging in chains required an especially made harness consisting of a series of three-inch iron links. The chain harness, supported by iron hoops, was then placed around the body and the corpse hoisted into place. It remained exposed until it rotted away. The gibbet upon which Kidd was exhibited was located not at Wapping but at Tilbury Point on the Thames. This was an excellent location, for ships sailing up and down the river could see the grisly corpse silhouetted against the sky.

Two hundred and twenty-nine years later, in January 1932, the dredger *Frederick* was operating near the place where Kidd dangled. They fished up a length of chain and an ancient padlock which was later identified by the authorities of the London Museum as part of a chain harness similar to that used on Kidd's body. The ironwork was definitely eighteenth century.

In a commentary on the demise of William Kidd, Harold T. Wilkins, an English writer, declared: "Captain William Kidd had died to save India for the British Empire! Yea, and in answer to many who may cavil at this statement of sheer historic fact, I would ask them to remember that the Great Mogul had threatened—and meant to be as good as his word—to come with an army and drive the East India Company and their factors out of India, unless, as his Imperial Highness said, the English pirates were hanged!" It is quite possible that the Great Mogul might have done just that.

Balladmongers in London's Grub Street quickly celebrated Kidd's death in long narrative poems which have survived to this day. One of the most interesting (and longest) deals with his adventures in the Red Sea and ends with this sad farewell:

> Farewell to young and old,
> All jolly seamen bold,
> You're welcome to my gold,
> For I must die, I must die.
> Farewell to Lunnon town,
> The pretty girls all round,
> No pardon can be found,
> And I must die, I must die.
> Farewell for I must die.
> Then to eternity, in hideous misery,
> I must lie, I must lie.

For months Kidd's body, hanging in chains, was exhibited at Tilbury Point on the Thames, as a warning to would-be pirates. (From The Pirates' Own Book.*)*

11

Hue and Cry

Until 1827 *hue and cry* was used in England and her colonies to signify the old common law process of pursuing a
criminal with horn and voice. It was the duty of any person
who had been robbed or who discovered a felony to raise
the hue and cry. His neighbors also were bound to turn out
with him and help discover the offender. Any one of those
engaged in the hue and cry could arrest the person pursued,
even though it turned out he was innocent. If he still had
about him evidence of guilt, such as stolen goods or money,
a swift fate was in store for him. If he resisted he could be
shot or cut down. When brought before a court, neither
was he allowed to say anything in self-defense nor was
there any need for accusation, indictment or appeal. Proof
was not required of a culprit's guilt, but merely that he had
been taken red-handed by hue and cry.

So it is quite understandable that whenever Red Sea Men returned to the American colonies, they were in immediate danger of capture by hue and cry.

An example of how one pirate-trader tried, by stealth, to avoid a hue and cry is that of Giles Shelley of the notorious ship *Nassau*. He reported his arrival in America in a letter to his employer, Stephen Delancey, dated at Cape May, May 27, 1699.[1] This was almost exactly a year to the day from the time Shelley had left New York with a ship loaded with trading goods and supplies for the pirates of Madagascar. His return cargo consisted of many bales of fine muslins and calicos, a ton of elephant ivory, opium, zinc, and Negro slaves.

Of his twenty-nine pirate passengers he wrote: "Most of them design for Virginia and the Hore Kills [a favorite pirate hideout near Lewes, Delaware] ... I have for the passage about twelve thousand pieces of eight and about three thousand Lyon Dollars ... make what dispatch you can for fear some of our Passengers should discover [reveal] us."

Regardless of Shelley's worry that he might be "discovered," his employer arranged for him to anchor at Sandy Hook, land his cargo at night and smuggle it into the well-guarded warehouses of pious Stephen Delancey. In spite of this secrecy, the news of Shelley's arrival with his rich cargo, pirate passengers and their personal loot sped through the colonies. Honest government officials were frantic. Merchants were ecstatic. It was said that Shelley's cargo was worth £50,000, estimated at $2,000,000 in today's value.

The pirates who landed at Cape May quickly spread through New Jersey. They were scared. They knew that their Arabian gold and bags of jewelry would immediately stamp them as Red Sea Men. They were from various vessels, all of which had engaged in piracy. Some had been the original crew of Kidd's ship the *Quedagh Merchant*, alias *Adventure Galley;* others had been followers of Robert Culliford and Richard Shivers of New England. Those who planned to hide out in Virginia went aboard a sloop belonging to an associate of Delancey. They set sail for the Virginia capes. After proceeding a short distance, they overtook a sloop, and Robert Bradenham (later to testify against Kidd) and three others transferred to the smaller vessel. Farther down the coast two more pirates transferred to a vessel bound for England. Later on others did the same. They all agreed that when they arrived in London they were to meet at the Flushing Pinck, a tavern near the Tower of London. By the time Shelley reached Sandy Hook, only seven of his original passengers were aboard.

Those who landed at Cape May had good reason to be afraid. Governor Bass of West Jersey had raised the hue and cry. He lost no time in appointing Judge Quarry of the Vice Admiralty Court to head the search, and capture the pirates. Quarry had authority in all the provinces. Meanwhile Governor Blakiston of Maryland was alerted and set a watch on all bays, inlets and creeks along the coast of his colony. Quarry also kept a sharp eye on Delaware Bay, having heard that Bradenham and his companions were somewhere in that area. But by the time Governor Bass had armed a sloop and loaded it with a crew of pirate hunters, the pirates had disappeared.

It was not only a matter of tracking down and capturing the sea robbers; it was also hard to keep them jailed. As long as the pirates had money, they had friends among the farmers and townsfolk. While the hue and cry was in progress, the pirates remained hidden but were well provided with good food and rum at an understandably high price. They were smuggled from place to place and tipped off when the authorities got too close.

The jails were anything but tight. They were usually small structures of wood and easy to break out of. Nevertheless two weeks after the *Nassau* had discharged its pirate passengers at Cape May, Governor Bass had four in custody, two of whom were captured by his men and two by Judge Quarry.

The next day the local sheriff complained to Bass that he could not guarantee keeping the pirates secure because the Quakers persisted in helping them.

The thirst for money was not confined to a particular group by any means. The Quakers (who preferred to be called members of the Society of Friends) were not immune to the opportunities for making money quickly and easily by trading with the pirates. As proof, a pamphleteer in 1703 declared: "These Quakers have a neat way of getting money by encouraging the pyrates, when they bring in good store of gold, so that when Avery's men were here in 1697, the Quaking justices were for letting them live quietly or else they were bailed easily."

Governor Bass was violently opposed to allowing bail for pirates who were caught and demanded that they be kept in strong confinement. It is a historical fact that in one instance the Quakers warned Judge Quarry that "If he raised ten men to put any of them [the pirates] into jail they would raise twenty more to get them out again." Apparently Quarry did not possess sufficient power from the Crown to force the Quakers to obey the law.

In another instance, a Jersey sheriff offered £10 to anyone who would capture a pirate. At that very moment, four fugitives were dining as the guests of Quakers Henry Grube and Elizabeth Bassett. They didn't stay long, for the sheriff was close behind. Later they were cornered and surrendered.

Finally, Governor Bass became so frustrated by people,

especially Quakers, conniving with the pirates that he gave up trying to keep them in jail and bailed most of them.[2]

In spite of Bass's energetic campaign the sum total of his arrests could hardly be called great; four pirates were under bail; two had escaped to Long Island; one was in hiding in Jersey, one had turned pirate again, and Darby Mullins was in prison.

Pirate loot seized and turned over to Judge Quarry amounted to $7800, thirty pounds of melted silver, gold coins both European and Arabian, cloth and jewelry. The score of Governor Markham of Pennsylvania was poor— only two pirates taken. But one of them, Bradenham, as stated before, was sent to London and testified against William Kidd. Bradenham had a considerable amount of treasure taken from him but had managed to conceal 2300 pieces of gold which he later took with him.

It is an open question why Governor Bass failed to do a good roundup job on the pirates. He blamed most of his failure on the Quakers, with whom he had waged a private war for some time. He claimed that the Quakers hid the pirates and aided them in every way to avoid the law. The members of the Society of Friends were certainly not alone in shielding the pirates. Religious affiliation had nothing to do with it. Pirates had money and were willing to give generous bribes and pay for protection. Any man with an itching palm was likely to help them.

The pirates jailed or bailed by Governors Bass of Jersey and Markham of Pennsylvania were only a small portion of the pirates ranging freely along the Atlantic seaboard. Some of Kidd's men were hiding out at the Hore Kills and the Delaware Bay area. Others left their shipmates and went on their own, hoping to escape detection. The number will never be known, but it ran well into the hundreds. Virtually all of them were Red Sea Men. Having been used to pillaging ashore on the Malabar Coast, it is not surprising that they made frequent raids along the Atlantic coast, robbing and pillaging and forcing shopkeepers to trade them rum, powder and shot and other necessities for gold and looted merchandise.

If Judge Quarry thought that things were hard in Jersey, he had a surprise waiting for him in Pennsylvania. Of all the colonies to which the Red Sea Men had scattered, Pennsylvania seemed to offer them safety and a warm welcome.

In the year 1699, the city of Philadelphia was twice as large as New York, with a population of approximately twelve thousand. The Pennsylvania Assembly was made up largely of conservative merchants. But there was a strong antagonism between two groups of different religious faiths: the Anglicans and the Quakers. They thoroughly despised each other, and each group took every opportunity to embarrass the other side. There was also a struggle between William Penn, the Proprietor, and the people, who were beginning more and more to assert their rights as free citizens.

At this time William Markham performed the duties of Acting Governor in the absence of William Penn, with the title of Lieutenant Governor. He had been in office since 1694. He and James Logan, Penn's secretary, were the active heads of the Proprietary Party, composed of leading Pennsylvania Quakers. It is a strange paradox that these respectable members of the Society of Friends, a religious body totally opposed to war and violence of any kind, should have tolerated the presence of pirates in Philadelphia and the surrounding area. To make matters worse, the Quakers had strongly opposed the formation of a body of militia, so that it was doubly difficult to round up Red Sea Men and guard them properly.

Penn's excuse that Markham was suffering from the gout

at the time and could not actively supervise the hue and cry against the pirates is hardly valid. He had no interest in the project or any desire to round up the rascals, especially since his daughter was married to James Brown, a notorious pirate captain. Nevertheless the Browns enjoyed the highest social distinction and mixed with the best of Philadelphia society.

Pennsylvania officials charged with capturing the pirates complained that Governor Markham was in league with the rascals and was surrounded by "evil men who gave the pirates intelligence and carried them off the country in boats."

The other faction in Pennsylvania, the Anglicans, had the pirate-chaser Judge Robert Quarry as its leader. Most of them were members of Christ Church, Philadelphia.

Since Quarry had been appointed an Admiralty Judge by the Crown of England he rightly felt himself superior to any local justices and was not in any way responsible to the Proprietor of Pennsylvania.

Markham's attitude toward the presence of freebooters in his province is well illustrated by the narrative[3] of Captain Robert Snead, one of the justices of the peace of Pennsylvania. It is too long to be quoted in full. In substance, here is what he related:

In April 1697, Snead received a copy of the Proclamation issued by the Lord Justices in Whitehall to arrest certain pirates that had arrived from Coruña, Spain, in the ship *Fancy*, alias *Charles the Second*. Henry Every, alias Bridgeman, was the commander. This man was actually John Avery, the notorious diamond-stealing pirate whose turgid life and ignominious death were described in Chapter 3. The pirates mentioned by Captain Snead were Robert Clinton, Edmund Lassel, Peter Claus (a cooper), and others who had slipped ashore at Cape May from Avery's ship before he went to Boston. From the record it seems that two of them were residents of Philadelphia.

Having ascertained that they had sneaked into town and knowing that Markham had seen a copy of the Proclamation, Snead went to him about the matter. Markham claimed he had not seen the Proclamation. Snead showed him his copy. After looking at it, Markham said that it was not directed to him, so that he was "not bound to take notice of it, nor to examine men from whence they came." Snead replied that the Proclamation was directed to all His Majesty's governors in the plantations and all officers and persons whatsoever and that Markham, being Governor, should execute it for his own safety and to satisfy the Crown authorities. They were bound to know, sooner or later, that pirates were parading up and down the streets of Penn's "greene country towne." Markham replied in effect that, if the matter was so important, the Lord Justices should have written him direct.

"I being at y^t time very Intimate with him [Markham] told him very plainly that there was a good understanding between him and ye Pyrates, & none so blind as those y^t would not see."

Markham admitted that the sea rovers had been "civil to him" and declared that since they had brought in money, it was an advantage to the province.

Snead was so disgusted at this remark that "I then asked him how I could be discharged from my oath as a Magistrate, if I did not take notice of ye proclamaçon. He was very angry & upon that I left him."

During this interchange, Markham's wife and daughter (wife of Pirate Brown) had been eavesdropping. Snead found out that they "heard what passed between ye Gov'r and myself, & went to Robert Clinton, one of the pyrates, & told the rest of ye Pyrates of it, whereupon they were so impudent as to call me inform^r as I pass't ye streets: I again went to the Govern^r & acquainted him of their Insolency,

& that I believed some of his family had acquainted the pyrates of our discourse about them; His wife and Daughter (then being in the room) say'd they did hear it, & that I was no better than an Inform^r & deserved to be so call'd; I then told him what was discoursed in his house in private relating to the publick ought not to be divulged, his answer was that he gave me no thanks for it. I then told him that I was resolved, by the help of God to apprehend those Pyrates according to ye proclamaçon, and that I would not be forsworne to oblige him and so left him."

From this it appears that even the good Quaker ladies of Philadelphia, dazzled by the presents of gold and gems and precious fabrics from their pirate relatives and friends, were as eager to protect them from the law as their husbands and fathers!

Now thoroughly incensed but determined, Captain Snead went separately to Edward Shippen and Anthony Maurice, two of his fellow justices, told them about the proclamation and asked their assistance in arresting the pirates. Snead talked to Maurice first, for while the distraught magistrate was conferring with Shippen, Maurice hurried over to Governor Markham and had a secret conference with him. When he returned to Snead he "refused to act, pretending he had other Business."

Maurice's reluctance to go pirate-grabbing is understandable. His kinswoman was married to Peter Claus, one of the very pirates Snead was after. This fact did not deter Snead: "Upon my threatening to Complaine of him at Whitehall, he then joyned with us."

At this point, it would seem that honest Magistrate Snead's popularity rating in Philadelphia society touched zero. He had committed the unpardonable sin in meddling in "family affairs."

Nevertheless the pirates were arrested and examined. Lassel, Clinton and Claus were proved to have been members of Avery's crew, while Brown (Markham's son-in-law) claimed he was merely a passenger. Yet it was well known that he was a Red Sea Man. Snead was for "committing them to close prison." But Shippen and Maurice argued that the men should be bailed. A legal wrangle ensued. The pirates were finally jailed, but only for a very short time, for Snead reported in his narrative that "soon after they were at liberty, & went to their own houses, and into the Countrey for Severall days together." A happy family weekend, no doubt.

Snead was in for more trouble from Quaker Lieutenant Governor Markham. When Snead issued warrants for the arrest of other known pirates, Markham sent the sheriff to Snead, demanding what right he had to issue warrants without informing him (Markham) for he was the Chief Justice and that Snead should "not send my warrants up & down whistling to scare people (meaning the Pyrates)." Markham also demanded to know what evidence Snead had against them, saying that they were not to be kept in prison merely for his pleasure. Snead replied that the King's Evidence was ready when a legal court was appointed to try the pirates, but refused to tell Markham what he had to prove against them.

The Acting Governor angrily called Snead a "Rascall" and warned him not to send out his warrants, adding that he had a good mind to commit Snead to jail. Markham also instructed the constables not to serve any more warrants. They obeyed.

Still fuming, Markham issued a warrant in his own handwriting, this time directed to the sheriff of Philadelphia, ordering him to disarm Captain Snead. "I liv'd 5 miles out of town," Snead wrote, "and was often threatened by those

Pyrates & did at y^t times ride armed for my Defense, for they were at Liberty; Curtis ye undersheriff accordingly served the warrant, & took from me my Sword and Pistolls . . . and left me to ride home without any Arms, keeping them till the Pyrates were Gone."

Soon afterwards Markham called his Council together and told them what a pity it was for the pirates to languish in jail and asked them to consider how a trial could be arranged. The Council candidly told Markham that they knew of no power sufficient in America to try the sea rovers, nor did the Council want any part of the business. They said that the best answer to the pirate problem was to load the rogues aboard a British man-of-war and send them to London to be tried. Markham said that he didn't need their advice for that and, "seemingly displeased," dismissed his advisers.

Then came, direct to Markham's hand, an official copy of the Lord Justices' proclamation, for which he was required to give a receipt. Two hours later the sheriff hurried from the Governor's mansion to the jail and had a long conference with the pirates.

Meanwhile Snead went to Markham and told him that if his prison was not strong enough to hold the pirates, "I would ord^r him a sufficient watch to guard them but he say'd he would doe well enough with 4 of them but Clinton and Lassel . . . made their Escape that night . . . the others continued in Gaole . . . but a little time after those pyrates which remained in prison had their liberty without Bayle."

In desperation, Captain Snead begged Markham for a warrant and a posse to apprehend Lassel and Clinton, "but nothing was done about it." The last heard of the two rogues was that they had sailed for Carolina. Peter Claus (kinsman of Justice Maurice) and James Brown (Markham's son-in-law) seem to have settled down in the bosom of their families, to enjoy their Red Sea loot in the "City of Brotherly Love."

In spite of Markham's lack of co-operation, Judge Quarry vigorously pursued the pirates in the Delaware Bay area, while Governor Bass was tracking down his culprits in Jersey. Markham had coldly refused Judge Quarry's request for the use of a sloop and forty men to rout out the nest of pirates snugly ensconced on the west side of Delaware Bay. Furious, Quarry acted on his own. He commandeered a sloop, and drummed up a crew of resolute men who were attracted by the high pay of seven shillings a day.

But all of the good judge's efforts produced miserable results. By this time the pirates had scattered and it was like trying to find the proverbial needle in a haystack. Quarry dejectedly estimated that the treasure owned by these fugitives was worth at least thirty thousand pounds. No doubt the judge wished with all his heart that honest William Penn had been on hand to give him assistance. But Penn did not arrive until December 1699, six months after the hue and cry against the Red Sea Men had begun.

Quarry's score then stood at eight pirates apprehended, finally including Kidd's notorious surgeon, Bradenham. One of the pirates had with him 4700 pieces of eight. Another, who had 2300 gold coins, broke out of jail leaving only a small amount of his treasure behind.

The influence of the Red Sea Men on the province of Pennsylvania was deplorable. Their easy money and cheerful disregard of the law, their violence in rescuing goods that had been seized from them and their frequent assaults on the King's officers led to almost a complete moral breakdown of the community. The situation was referred to by an upright individual at the time who asked, "what would law abiding sailors do when they, coming heather & seeing

pyrates & murderers at liberty, respected & made the companions of ye best and masters of such great sumes of
money are encouraged to turn villains too."

Hardly a Red Sea Man in Pennsylvania would have been
shipped to London for trial had not William Penn fortunately arrived in his province during the last month of
1699. Meanwhile, it would be well to take another look at
that wily rogue "Doctor" Robert Bradenham, who later
helped send Captain Kidd to the gallows. He was a glib
fellow, pompous, and a good actor, who could put on a
cloak of respectability that fooled a good many people.
William Penn dubbed him "an ingenious fellow pretending
great innocence and honor." Bradenham realized, of course,
that as a member of Kidd's crew, he was under grave suspicion. He declared unctuously that it was his misfortune
and not his crime to have sailed with Kidd. Bradenham figured that since his chances of being shipped to London for
trial were excellent, he had better place his loot in reliable
hands to be picked up later if he was lucky enough to
escape the hangman's noose.

At this time Reverend Edward Porlock was rector of
Christ Church in Philadelphia.[4] After being released from
jail on bail, Bradenham called on the clergyman, claiming
to be an honest seaman (which even the rector knew he
wasn't) who wished to place his life savings in responsible hands. He asked the rector to take charge of part of his
treasure. This consisted of 624 gold coins worth at that time
approximately £414. At today's valuation the money would
be worth at least ten times that amount. A tidy fortune. The
Reverend Edward Porlock was well known and admired in
Philadelphia for his sermons which thundered Hell and
Damnation to Sinners. One of his favorite targets was the
Quakers and "other instruments of the Devil" who consorted with pirates.

What more honest gentleman could be chosen, thought Bradenham, as a repository for his gold than this eminent divine? Porlock apparently came under the spell of Bradenham's tales of adventure, for they became sufficiently intimate that Penn "found the parson potting and piping with him [Bradenham] and the other pirates at the time I went myself to see them . . ." Potting and piping meant that the clergyman was drinking pots of ale and smoking pipes of tobacco with his new-found pirate friends.

But Bradenham was too smart to put all his gold coins into one clergyman's basket. The other repository was the broad, hamlike hand of a certain Charles Sober, who was told to deliver two small rolls of gold coins to William Hall of Philadelphia, who styled himself "innkeeper and practitioner of Physick."

These illicit transactions were well concealed until William Penn began an investigation. He was suspicious of Bradenham and became even more so when he was informed by a certain person, name unknown, that the Reverend Edward Porlock had in his possession 624 pieces of gold which Bradenham had entrusted to him before being shipped to England for trial.

Apparently Penn had a jaundiced view of the Reverend Mr. Porlock's dedication to fire and brimstone. He considered the sermons against pirates and other evildoers much overdone.

When the Reverend Mr. Porlock received a summons from Penn to appear for questioning in connection with his association with Bradenham, the rector was frightened. But his friends assured him that this was merely a routine matter and that he should deny everything. When Penn asked him about Bradenham's gold, Porlock shrugged and said he knew nothing about it. He had none of it in his keeping. Yet it was very evident to the rector that Penn did not be-

lieve him. Porlock was worried. It was noised about Philadelphia that Penn was collecting more evidence against the
rector. Finally Porlock could stand the suspense no longer.
Suddenly and stealthily he left the City of Brotherly Love,
with Bradenham's gold well secured about his own ecclesiastical person. Penn notified Governor Blakiston of Maryland to watch for the absconding minister, but he eluded all
search and ended up as rector of a small church in Kent
County, Maryland. Some wag in Philadelphia remarked
that "It takes a parson to cheat a Pyrate."

William Penn possessed not only a strong sense of right
and wrong but also a measure of humor. He rather enjoyed
the experience with the rector and even though he never
recovered Brandenham's money he always liked to repeat
the incident, pointing out how pirate gold could debauch
even a member of the clergy. In a letter to Governor Blakiston, "I waved to write anything to the Disadvantage of the
Parson, when Bradenham went home, apprehending the
disadvantage I lay under of being believed . . . The Bishop
of London should be spoke to by ye K [King] to use his
Ecclesiastic power with the parson."[5] Whether the Bishop
did so, deponent sayeth not.

Penn endured considerable criticism for his handling of
the Porlock case. Merchants and politicians reviled him for
being too severe. These were the very men who themselves
had traded with the pirates and were worried lest Penn
should stifle all trade and contact with the Red Sea Men.

In a document called *Pedigree of Piracy*, William Penn
wrote rather smugly, "I must needs say that Jamaica . . .
was the seminary, where pirates have commenced the Master of Arts, after having practiced upon the Spaniard (as
Privateers) and then launched for the Red and Arabian
Seas, and at Madagascar (or St. Mary's) and have found a
yearly supply of flour and ammunition from some of our

colonies . . . they have perhaps in ten years time got a million by it, but . . . we never had a spot on our garments." What he meant was that he never had a spot on his own garment, which hardly could be said of his gouty deputy, Markham, or dozens of other Quaker officials and merchants.

Although William Penn, already a wealthy man, resisted temptation, the great influx of gold and silver and shiploads of rare merchandise were a great enticement to men of high estate to flout the law. Most of them did not consider it a sin to buy goods stolen from Mohammedan infidels. Many a merchant and upright churchgoer who had thought himself to be scrupulously honest until the advent of the Red Sea Men could find many such excuses for dealing with them, especially if it meant handsome profits.

Meanwhile, in New York, the antagonism to Lord Bellomont continued. It was not confined to colonial merchants by any means. London businessmen were also against him. They drew up a list of thirty-two accusations, including the complaint that he was using excessive zeal in tracking down individuals who were thought to have received some of Kidd's goods and of hounding men suspected of doing business with him in the Red Sea.

The length to which these merchants and officials went to strew the Earl's path with broken glass is amazing to us today. The honest Attorney General of New York was threatened with death and the Regent of the Crown was persecuted. Even the mail directed to the Earl was intercepted for as much as a year. Bellomont's messengers were waylaid and beaten.

The extent of the corruption which had fastened itself in the highest places of the colony is demonstrated by the fact that Reverend William Vesey, who, at the time, was Rector of Trinity Church, New York, and Dominie Godfriedus Dellius of Albany publicly denounced Lord Bellomont for vacating the great grants of land made by Fletcher to his cronies.

What of Giles Shelley, successful pirate-trader and right-hand man of Delancey? After 100 per cent lack of co-operation from local authorities, Bellomont finally got him lodged in jail. When the Council met to consider his case, Attorney General James Graham declared at the morning session that Shelley certainly should be tried for piracy. But to everyone's astonishment, in the afternoon the Attorney General completely reversed himself, as did the Council. Graham declared that the Governor, even with all the power delegated to him by the Crown, could not prosecute Shelley unless he could produce witnesses who could prove Shelley a pirate. Not a single witness could be found. Shelley went free.

Again, as so many, many times before and since, cold cash in the right hands had triumphed over law and order. Bellomont was raging. In writing to the Lords of Trade, he declared that Shelley had "so flushed them at New York with Arabian gold and East Indian goods that the government was being outrageously defied."

A year after Shelley had bribed his way out of trouble in New York he was seen operating on the London stock exchange. Yet he was under suspicion by Admiralty lawyers. They had not forgotten Governor Bellomont's letters describing Shelley's insolent landing of pirates and pirate loot on the very front door of the Port of New York and his atrocious bribery.

At last they succeeded in indicting him for selling arms and powder to his friends at St. Mary, declaring that he had transported them from New York to Madagascar aboard his vessel the *Nassau* in June of 1698. But to everyone's astonishment, including Bellomont's, Shelley was found guilty of only a misdemeanor and released.

The slippery fellow returned to New York and apparently settled down to the life of a merchant, for we hear no more of him in the official records. No doubt he lived out his life behind a façade of respectability.

Second only to Shelley in nerve and insolence were "Doctor" Robert Bradenham and his shipmate, Theophilus Turner. As described before, Bradenham escaped hanging because he gave damaging testimony against Kidd. Turner cheated the noose by appearing against veteran Culliford, late of the *Mocha*. In spite of Turner's best efforts to arrange a hempen collar for his old friend, Culliford received the King's Pardon, due to the intercession of Captain Warren of the Royal Navy. Warren had gone to Madagascar to offer pardons to the nests of pirates there. Culliford had persuaded a number of them to submit. His pay for this was a pardon for himself.

After Bradenham and Turner were off the hook, they had the brass to petition the Admiralty for return of their treasure. They declared that they had been of great use to the Crown in connection with the trials of Kidd and Culliford and therefore deserved to have their booty returned to them. Surprisingly, the Admiralty consented, but first deducted the expenses of their board and keep during the lengthy trials. Bradenham and Turner received about half of the value of their original loot.

It was said that Bradenham returned to the Red Sea and to his old trade of piracy. Turner became a constable in London. His only distinction in that job was imprisoning the wrong person for piracy. He was fined six pounds, three shillings for his stupidity.

No doubt the persistent tales of pirate gold buried along the shore of New Jersey originated with two Red Sea Men, Howe and Churchill. These two scamps had caused Governor Bass no end of trouble by hiding among the swamps and woods of south Jersey. It was they who tried to con-

vince him that they could go over to St. Mary and dissolve
the colony by reforming the pirates and bringing them back
to lead respectable lives.

Bass, of course, refused and they were sent to London to
be tried. Although they admitted to piracy they declared
that they had submitted to the King's Pardon by coming to
Governor Bass. Yet at that time he had no legal power to
confer the King's Pardon on them. In any case, they were
allowed to go free, because at the last moment, Governor
Bass interceded for them. Since they had caused him so
much trouble, this is somewhat of a surprise. These rascals
immediately returned to New Jersey and dug up more than
£2000 in gold and silver which they had buried in the
woods. Did Governor Bass receive a handsome present for
helping them go free? Who knows?

What of Robert Livingston, the highly respected merchant and landowner who started the whole sordid and
bloody Kidd affair with his scheme to destroy piracy and at
the same time make a fortune? Being a canny Scot, Livingston remained discreetly silent during and after Kidd's trial
and death. He successfully kept out of the glare of publicity, for he was in America and could become conveniently obscure among his vast estates.

Nevertheless, the Kidd business made a heavy impact on
him. He was filled with mortification that his carefully nur-
tured reputation had been a bit tarnished. This is brought
out in a letter from Bellomont to Lord Somers, a member of
the defunct syndicate, dated March 7, 1700, from Boston:

> Mr. Livingstone is fallen into a fit of melancholy, and has
> removed from Albany to a farm he has between that and
> New York, resolving to meddle no more with business and
> that because his wife and relations are frightened out of their
> wits at his bond's lying for Kidd . . . I desire you will consent
> to my giving him up the bond and articles . . . Mr. Living-

stone, when he was here, was heartily troubled and ashamed at Kidd's villainous behaviour, and to reflect that he had been the means of engaging you and the rest of us to be concerned with that *monster;* which truly put me in charity with Mr. Livingstone and that he had no design to harm us, but was deceived as we . . .

From this it would appear that Mr. Livingston shed a bucketful of crocodile tears and that the main reason for his grief was that he got nothing but trouble for recommending Kidd.

Finally, what of Richard Coote, Lord Bellomont? He did not outlive Kidd, the man he hounded to the gallows, by more than three months. His wife, Kate, in a letter to Secretary of State James Vernon, wrote a fitting epitaph: "He wore out his spirrits and put an end to his life by the fatigue he hourly underwent to serve His Majestie in this country."

Poor Bellomont was not only worn out when he died, he was virtually bankrupt. At the end, the Council of New York performed at least one decent act for the man they hated: they rendered him military honors and paid his funeral expenses. Neither Bellomont nor his lady nor his heirs ever received a single penny from the Crown for the large expenditures made by the Earl in rounding up the scores of pirates and sending them to England for trial.

Lord Bellomont was buried in the chapel of the fort which at that time stood near the Battery on lower Manhattan. An unhappy destiny refused to let him rest in peace. In 1788 when the old fort was taken down and the site leveled, the wreckers came upon an ancient Dutch vault containing the remains of Lord and Lady Bellomont. They were in leaden coffins, identified by Bellomont's escutcheon and the engraving on the silver coffin plates. These coffins, with the bones of several unknown persons found nearby, were taken to St. Paul's churchyard, where they were placed in a common grave. Historian John F. Watson, in his *Annals and Occurrences of New York City and State*, published in 1846, says that the Bellomont bones were interred "without any notice above ground of 'storied urn or animated bust.' The silver plates were taken . . . for a museum . . . but they later fell into hands which with much bad taste, converted them into spoons."

There was little of a constructive nature that resulted from Bellomont's brief term as Governor. His administration was marred by a running fight with his Council and most of the merchants and officials, few of whom he could trust. His main contribution was breaking the strong grip of the Red Sea Men and reducing the trade in stolen merchandise throughout the American colonies. Although piracy continued along the Atlantic coast and in the Red Sea area for nearly a quarter of a century after Bellomont's death, it steadily diminished. Meanwhile colonial merchants developed legitimate trade with the prosperous West Indian Islands under the British flag, which brought them steady and smaller but legal profits.

This romanticized picture of Kidd burying part of his treasure on Gardiner's Island, by Howard Pyle, is inaccurate in two respects: the sword he is wearing was not made until 150 years later, and the wooden chest would soon have rotted away if left buried for any length of time.

12

What Happened to Captain Kidd's Treasure?

THE *Quedagh Merchant*, captured by Captain Kidd, was a large vessel of five hundred tons burden, which meant she was capable of carrying a *cargo* weighing five hundred tons. Even a great quantity of East Indian merchandise such as silks, muslins, calicoes, madras, cloth of gold and silver, as well as gold dust, silver bullion, gems and jewelry are light in weight compared to their value. In addition, the *Quedagh Merchant* carried a certain amount of sugar, iron and saltpeter and general merchandise. Authorities differ on the total value of the ship and cargo, but the most conservative estimate is £400,000 or $2,000,000 *in 1698*. This does not tell the whole story by any means, because the purchasing power of the pound in 1698 was far, far greater than it is today. It is safe to say that the value of the *Quedagh Merchant* and her cargo, according to today's purchasing power, would be close to £4,000,000 or $11,200,000, figuring the pound at its present par value of $2.80.

After his seizure of the *Quedagh Merchant*, Kidd's immediate problem was to find the best ways and means for disposing of the vast amount of cargo. The gold, jewels and silver were no problem, of course. But the bulky merchandise and the sugar and iron and saltpeter had to be got rid of as soon as possible.

Like the businessmen of New York and Philadelphia, and other Atlantic ports, the merchants of the west coast of India were eager to buy up captured merchandise for a shilling or less in the pound. As we have seen, Kidd had no trouble in disposing of part of his cargo to these eager traffickers in stolen merchandise, and in cheating them as well.

The refusal of the Danish governor of St. Thomas to allow Kidd to remain there upset his plans, for it is certain that he never intended to sail the *Quedagh Merchant* to New York or Boston at this time. Nor did Kidd dare risk asking for sanctuary at any of the British, Spanish, or Dutch islands, for all their governors had received notices of Kidd's piracies and were asked to keep a sharp eye out for him and immediately notify the British navy.

Kidd had to make up his mind in a hurry and he did so. He left the *Quedagh Merchant* in charge of Henry Bolton,[1] an Englishman and former customs and excise collector of the British island of Antigua. Bolton's past was none too savory. He had been discharged from his post, owing the Crown £500, a large sum in those days. Whether Kidd knew this when he made his deal with Bolton is unknown. But it is quite likely that Kidd had known Bolton during his old privateering days in the Caribbean.

Kidd's plan was to sequester the *Quedagh Merchant* at some lonely spot in the West Indies until he had cleared himself of the charge of piracy. He would then have her condemned as a prize, using one of his French passes as proof that she was a legal capture. Then he would refit her and sail north to New York, his home port, where the remainder of her cargo would be sold at high prices for the benefit of himself, Bellomont, Livingston and the others of the syndicate.

Believing that he had left the *Quedagh Merchant* in honest and capable hands, Kidd purchased the sloop *Antonio*, loaded aboard his personal treasure and some merchandise, and headed north with the remnants of his crew and passengers. Although the colonial records refer to the *Antonio* as a sloop, she was probably a vessel of good size, for ships of considerable tonnage were called sloops in those days.

Kidd in the *Antonio* and Bolton in the *Quedagh Merchant* sailed together to an obscure creek on the island of Hispaniola (now the republics of Haiti and Santo Domingo). The place was known as Santa Catalina. The caretaker crew left aboard the *Quedagh Merchant* consisted of eighteen men, some of whom had been pirates in Madagascar.

At Kidd's trial the testimony about the exact location of the *Quedagh Merchant* varied widely. Three different locations were sworn to by members of Kidd's crew, themselves on trial for piracy.

After Bolton had been tracked down, captured and sent to London for trial for receiving stolen goods, he made a deposition in which he described what happened after Kidd sailed north in the *Antonio*. Bolton's story was discovered some twenty-five years ago among the manuscripts of the Duke of Portland at Welbeck Abbey. Here is Bolton's story:

> Kidd's seamen [caretaker crew], after his departure plundered the best and the most choicest goods he had left behind. This came to my knowledge, after they had been near

five weeks aboard [the *Quedagh Merchant*], but I could do nothing against eighteen men, because there was only myself and a Negro boy to oppose them. The eighteen men broke into open mutiny as the time was drawing nigh when they might expect Kidd to return. They swore to me that they would not stay in the ship, being terrified of Kidd's returning. All of them except the boatswain came on the quarterdeck and said to me: "You can remain in the ship and be damned. We stay no longer!" I pushed the man who said this down the steps to the quarterdeck and ordered the rest to return to their duties. I was resolved to stay till the twelve months were up and I told Kidd's men if they did not I would write to all the governments in those parts to have them secured. This calmed them down for two or three dayes. Next thing I heard was they drew up a round robin, signed their names in the circle, and directed it to me, setting forth their resolution to leave the ship. So they gott aboard another sloope and went to the island of Curaçao, leaving me and three more in the ship. I stayed a week in the ship and then left, hearing that the Spaniards in St. Domingo were arming out a brigantine to come and take us. I left the *Adventure Prize* [Kidd's alias for the *Quedagh Merchant*] in the Rio Higuey, moored to stumps and went to Curaçao to get satisfaction of the seamen who had three hundred pounds to four hundred pounds a man. The governor would not admit me to this Dutch island, though John Ware [Kidd's master of the ship] and Kidd's seamen were there under his [the Dutch governor's] protection. I did not charge this to the governor (who is since dead) for I should be very sorry to disturb the ashes of so good a Gentleman as I believe he was, but on some of his council that did not desire I should face them.

Bolton declared at his trial that all he got for his trouble was £308 in pieces of eight from the sale of Kidd's goods, "all the rest is debts outstanding, which is much less than my charges."

That Bolton was lying was proved by Governor Bello-mont who declared he had evidence that Henry Bolton got £16,000 from looting the *Quedagh Merchant*.

According to responsible persons in London, Bolton proved to be "a cunning and brazen rogue who wore a cloak of piety."

As for the *Quedagh Merchant*, she came to an inglorious end. How or why she was set afire remains a mystery. Some say she was burned to the waterline at Kidd's orders, fearing that the very existence of the vessel would hurt his defense. The vessel was stripped clean before she was set on fire. Whatever remained of her guns and fittings were taken by the people of that section of Hispaniola, now part of the republic of Haiti. Unfortunately certain documents and relics would have been preserved to this day except that they were destroyed during the Negro revolt in the spring of 1804.

Although Bolton was undoubtedly dishonest, it is certain, from the evidence brought out at his trial, that he made some serious attempts to dispose of the *Quedagh Merchant's* cargo, particularly on the Dutch island of Curaçao. He claimed that many of the merchants to whom he consigned the merchandise failed to pay for it. On the contrary, one witness declared that Bolton pocketed £100,000 from his transactions with the *Quedagh Merchant's* cargo. But Bolton responded, "I wish it were ten thousand pounds, but do not believe it will amount to near that sum, for the persons to whom I sent and consigned the goods have robbed and defrauded me of the greater part thereof."

Through generous use of his ill-gotten gains, Bolton managed to get himself bailed out of jail. From there he disappears into the mists of anonymity.

Now to return to the *Antonio* and Captain Kidd sailing north to his doom. How much Kidd's merchandise and his own personal treasure aboard the sloop amounted to is anyone's guess. It was said to be worth upwards of one hundred thousand pounds or approximately one quarter of the total value of the *Quedagh Merchant* and her cargo.

There is strong evidence that Kidd consistently undervalued the *Quedagh Merchant's* cargo and his own share of the loot. This is understandable, since he realized that if the charge of piracy was made to stick, he would not stand much chance of recovering any of the merchandise or treasure if seized by officials of the colonies.

Lord Bellomont later declared that when Kidd came north, his cargo and treasure was worth seventy thousand pounds. He also stated that Kidd had falsified his accounts to make it appear less. On the other hand, Judge Samuel Sewall, who made an official inventory of treasure and merchandise belonging to Kidd which was unloaded at Boston, said it came to a mere fourteen thousand pounds.

Sewall's inventory included gold dust, coin gold, coin silver, silver rings, precious stones, unpolished stones, silver buttons, and gold and silver bars.

It was this treasure that Kidd buried on Gardiner's Island in a field known as the "Cherry Tree." Tradition says that he threatened to murder Gardiner and his family if they revealed where he had hid the booty. Later Gardiner, fearful for the lives of himself and family, required assurances from Lord Bellomont's commissioners that Kidd was safely locked up before he led the commissioners to the field to dig up the hidden treasure.

According to John Gardiner's deposition before Bellomont and his council, Kidd also landed a number of bales of goods and a Negro boy on Gardiner's Island. There was a tradition that Kidd made a present of some cloth of gold to Mrs. Gardiner and that a piece of it remained in the family for many years. This has never been confirmed. Surviving members of the Gardiner family deny the story.

At that time Kidd told Gardiner that the silver, gold and jewels he had buried were intended as a gift to Lord and Lady Bellomont. Gardiner estimated that the gold and silver in the chest weighed more than thirty pounds. But one of the commissioners, Isa Addington, noted that the treasure consisted of "a Boxe of fifty pounds of Gold and Plate."

From this time on, goods and treasure from Kidd's sloop were gradually distributed to various individuals he felt he could trust. Kidd was desperate. He wrote a letter to Captain Thomas Pain, a retired pirate, ordering Pain to give Mrs. Kidd twenty-four ounces of gold, "but keep the rest until further notice." Pain lived on an island in Narragansett Bay. When the Earl of Bellomont sent officers to search Pain's house they found he had stolen away "with a deal more of Kidd's goods still in his hands."

So intent were Bellomont and his minions on accounting for every penny of Kidd's treasure that they arrested Mrs. Kidd and her housekeeper, Dorothy Lee. Both women were questioned extensively while in custody for ten days. Everything of value that these women had, and which the officials thought might have come from Kidd, was seized. Among the stuff was Mrs. Kidd's own silverware, which Bellomont immediately ordered returned to her.

Another recipient of Kidd's largess was his friend Duncan Campbell, bookseller and postmaster of Boston. It was he who had attempted to pave the way for Kidd with Bellomont, unsuccessfully. Campbell received one hundred pieces of eight, together with an enameled box containing four gems set in gold, several other precious stones, and a Negro slave. In addition, when Campbell's mansion was searched, they found five bags of gold, one bag of silver and "a handkerchief of gold."

Another character who dipped his hands into Kidd's loot was "Whisking" Clarke, coroner of New York. How he got hold of the merchandise, no one can say, but he immediately locked it up in Major Salleck's warehouse near Stamford, Connecticut, and defied Bellomont to come and get it. His little cache was valued at between five thousand and twelve thousand pounds. Nevertheless, a short time later, Clarke was seized and delivered to the Lieutenant Governor of New York along with Kidd's goods.

In addition to all this, there were persistent rumors that Kidd had landed at various points along the Atlantic coast on his way north and buried a great deal of treasure. Innumerable places have their own pet legends about vast quantities of bar gold, silver, and pieces of eight buried in the woods or along the shore. It is certainly true that a number of Kidd's men *did* bury treasure. Howe and Churchill did, and dug it up again.

By the time Kidd was hanging in chains, the value of his treasure which actually reached London had shrunk to a pittance. Colonial officials deducted sizable amounts for expenses incurred for feeding and clothing Kidd and his men while in jail. There were also expenses in transporting the criminals to London for trial and more expenses in keeping their bodies and souls together during the full year which passed before the pirates were tried.

After Kidd's death, the remainder of his treasure was sold at public auction, on November 13, 1701, by decree of the High Court of the Admiralty. It consisted of several parcels of gold and silver, some diamonds and rubies, and bales of merchandise. The entire lot brought a mere £6472 and one shilling. Some time later Queen Anne granted the entire amount to the Royal Naval Hospital at Greenwich, which cared for disabled seamen. Thus, in the end, the small remnant of Kidd's treasure did some good!

One of the most surprising aspects of the era of the Red Sea Men was the attitude of colonial and Crown officials toward the merchandise and treasure captured from Indian

merchants and other subjects of the Great Mogul. The attitude can best be expressed this way: today, if a gang of
American criminals aboard an armed vessel captured a
richly laden ship belonging to citizens of the Republic of
Mexico, the American authorities would certainly make
every effort to return the goods to their rightful Mexican
owners after the criminals were taken into custody. Such a
practice was not followed in Kidd's day. In the view of the
British authorities, the duty of colonial officials was to track
down, capture and seize pirates, their treasure and merchandise. After deducting necessary expenses, the booty
was then forwarded to the Admiralty in London for dis-
position. But from all available records, it has been established that the Admiralty brushed off the pleas of the Indian
and Armenian merchants for the return of their property or
adequate compensation for their losses.

A petition dated July 17, 1701, by an Armenian merchant
named Cogi Babba declared that when Kidd captured the
Quedagh Merchant he threw overboard all the bills of lading and all the account books belonging to the merchants
and factors, in which they had listed the contents of each
of the bales and boxes of merchandise on board the vessel.

Cogi Babba also confirmed the story that Kidd had sold
a quantity of merchandise from the *Quedagh Merchant*,
including raw silks and opium to the value of about twenty
thousand pounds English money. Cogi Babba claimed that
Kidd was paid in gold bars and gold dust. Cogi Babba's petition also specified a great many of the precious stones and
gold which he lost when Kidd captured the *Quedagh Merchant*.

But Cogi Babba and all the other merchants who lost
their fortunes from Kidd's plundering never received one
penny from the British Crown. Their petitions remain yel-
lowed with time and dusty in the files of the Admiralty.

It is quite understandable that the immense flow of gold, silver and precious gems into the American colonies generated innumerable stories and legends about Captain Kidd, the Red Sea Men and buried treasure.

The *Pirates Own Book*, first published in Boston in 1837, sums up the situation:

> The report of his [Kidd's] having buried great treasure of gold and silver, which he actually did before his arrest, set the brains of all good people along the coast in ferment. There were rumors on rumors of great sums of money found here and there, sometimes in one part of the country, sometimes in another; of coins with Moorish inscriptions, doubtless spoils of his Eastern prizes. Some reported the treasure to have been buried in solitary, unsettled places about Plymouth and Cape Cod, but by degrees, various other parts, not only on the eastern coast, but along the shores of the Sound, and even Manhattan and Long Island, were gilded by these rumors.
>
> In fact, the vigorous measures of Lord Bellomont had spread sudden consternation among the pirates in every part of the provinces; they had secreted their money and jewels in lonely, out of the way places, about the wild shores of the sea coast, and dispersed themselves over the country, but the hand of justice prevented many of them from ever returning to regain their buried treasures, which remain to this day thus secreted and irrevocably lost. This is the cause of the most recent reports of trees and rocks bearing mysterious marks, supposed to indicate the spots where treasures lay hidden; and many have been the ransackings after the pirates' booty. A rocky place on the shores of Long Island, called Kidd's Ledge, has received great attention from the money diggers, but they have not yet discovered any treasures.

As the years went by, the legends multiplied. Here is a partial list of the places[2] on the Eastern seaboard where

Kidd or his men are supposed to have hidden loot: Stamford, Stratford Point, Fishers Island, Block Island, Lime, Weathersfield, Thimble Island, Money Island, Squirrel Island, Cliff Island, Jewels Island, Isle au Haut, Halowell, Monhegan Island, Penobscot Bay, Penobscot River, Wiscasset, Frankfort, Deer Island, Cheshire, Conant's Island, Hog Island, Turner's Falls, Rye Pond, Rye, Cape May, Cliffwood, Sleepy Hollow, West Point, Putnam County, Stony Point, Canonicut Island, Bellows' Falls and practically all of the three hundred islands in Casco Bay.

It is also said that the mysterious treasure of Oak Island in Mahone Bay, Nova Scotia, was buried in its hundred-foot pit by Kidd and his men. The most unlikely treasure story concerns a mysterious island in the South China Sea.[3] This yarn was started in 1932 by an Englishman, Hubert Palmer, who claimed that he had discovered a chart in a treasure chest, said to have belonged to Captain Kidd. That Kidd would choose a spot so far away from home to bury his loot hardly makes sense.

Poor Captain William Kidd, they wouldn't let him lie. As someone put it, he was "tongue wagged to infamy." His career fired authors, dramatists and poets to make him the hero or the villain of innumerable fanciful productions. Famous writers, including Washington Irving, Robert Louis Stevenson, Edgar Allan Poe, and James Fenimore Cooper, helped create the legends that surround Kidd's name. Irving's story, "Money Diggers," even makes Captain Kidd responsible for the bloody deeds of a number of other pirates, including Henry Morgan and Blackbeard.

Even Harriet Beecher Stowe, author of the immortal *Uncle Tom's Cabin*, tried her hand at a blood-and-thunder tale with a gory story in the November, 1870, *Atlantic Monthly*, entitled "Captain Kidd's Money."

Of all the tales of pirates and hidden doubloons and

pieces of eight, none is better known or better loved than Stevenson's *Treasure Island*. He admitted that he had drawn on a number of other works for many of *Treasure Island's* details. He definitely had Kidd and the Red Sea Men in mind when writing his immortal pirate tale.

Modern science has now taken a hand in the hunt for pirate treasure by supplying efficient metal locators, sonar equipment, and various electronic devices for locating metal beneath the waves or underground. Several spectacular caches of treasure have been discovered in Bermuda, Nassau, and along the Florida coast by scuba divers who have made a serious study of the locations of sunken galleons and lost treasures. The results of their efforts, now on view in museums in Bermuda, Nassau, Florida, and the Smithsonian Institution in Washington, are fascinating, for they bring to life the old swashbuckling days of piracy and buried gold.

There is no doubt that at least part of Captain Kidd's treasure remains buried *somewhere*. It may not be much, but as the old saying goes, "Gold is where you find it."

When the glamour and romance and legend have been stripped from the Red Sea Men and their voyages, some basic facts stand out. The sudden wealth they poured into the American colonies had a powerful effect on the economy, on politics, and on moral standards. The selfishly motivated Navigation Acts of the British government which prohibited colonial merchants from trading with any other nations except the mother country greatly encouraged smuggling, piracy and widespread traffic in stolen goods. Even after piracy was largely suppressed, smuggling continued at a steady pace—to the very end of the Revolutionary War. During that period, particularly, smuggling was looked upon as a patriotic duty and privilege and was engaged in by some of the most respectable patriots.

The impact of the Red Sea Men on the political situation in the colonies was heavy. Although bribery and corruption were certainly not unknown before the advent of the pirates, the pinnacle was reached under the administration of Governor Benjamin Fletcher. Fortunately, as in so many other periods of history, the mills of the gods ground exceeding fine though slow. Thanks to Lord Bellomont's honest and active administration, upright colonial government was reinstated.

Today, the era of the Red Sea Men continues to be of interest, not only as a facet of history replete with temptation and greed, but also as a period that spawned as colorful a crew of cutthroats as ever went a-roving.

Notes

Chapter I—PIRACY WAS BIG BUSINESS

1. The word Viking means *pirate* or *sea rover* in Old Norse.

Chapter III—CAPTAIN JOHN AVERY, RED SEA CHAMPION

1. Avery's capture of *The Duke* and his dialogue in this chapter are based on *A History of the Robberies and Murders of the Most Notorious Pirates,* by Captain Charles Johnson, London, 1724.

Chapter IV—PIRATE EMPIRE

1. *The History of Piracy*, by Philip Gosse, New York, 1934.
2. *Piracy Was a Business*, by Cyrus H. Karraker, Rindge, N. H., 1953.
3. *The Memoirs of a Buccaneer*, by Louis Le Golif. Translated by Malcolm Barnes. George Allen and Unwin, Ltd., Ruskin House, London, 1961.
4. *The Scourge of the Indies*, by Maurice Besson (from original texts), New York, 1929.

Chapter V—WEAPONS, WOMEN AND WINE

1. *The Scourge of the Indies*, as above.
2. *The Memoirs of a Buccaneer*, as above.
3. *Ibid.*

Chapter VII—LIBERTATIA—PIRATE REPUBLIC

1. A glass means an hourglass which ran for a half hour.
2. Captain Misson's memoirs, written in French in manuscript form, were presumably saved by a member of his crew. They passed through several hands and were finally given to Captain Charles Johnson by "a friend and correspondent." Misson's memoirs and the authentic source of information about his life and exploits are described in Johnson's *A General History of the Most Notorious Pirates,* published in London, 1724.

Chapter VIII—WILLIAM KIDD, MERCHANT CAPTAIN

1. *The Real Captain Kidd,* by Cornelius Dalton, New York, 1911.
2. *Captain Kidd and His Skeleton Island,* by Harold T. Wilkins, London, 1935.
3. Kidd was mistaken about the lack of ships.
4. Now the capital of the Virgin Islands of the United States.
5. The "four great personages": Sir Edward Russell, First Lord of the Admiralty (later Lord Orford); Sir John Somers, Lord Keeper of the Great Seal; the Duke of Shrewsbury, Secretary of State; the Earl of Romney, Master-General of Ordnance.

Chapter IX—WILLIAM KIDD, PIRATE

1. *Documents Relative to the Colonial History of New York, IV.* All subsequent correspondence between Bellomont and the Lords of Trade is from the same source.
2. Quoted by H. T. Wilkins in *Captain Kidd and His Skeleton Island,* above.
3. *The Memoirs of Père Labat, 1693–1705,* translated and abridged by John Eaden, Constable & Co., Ltd., London, 1931.
4. Labat probably meant Mecca.

Chapter X—WILLIAM KIDD, GALLOWS BAIT

1. The fact that Wright was a British subject told heavily against Kidd at his trial.
2. All quotations from Kidd's trial are from the actual testimony as published in *The Arraignment, Tryal and Condemnation of Captain William Kidd,* London, 1701.
3. At this time was published in London *A Full Account of the Proceedings in Relation to Captain Kidd in Two Letters, Written by a Person of Quality to a Kinsman of the Earl of Bellomont in Ireland.* Much of what we know about what went on during the period of Kidd's trial, along with the gossip of the coffeehouses, is based on this publication.
4. Navy Board Minutes, April 14, 1700.
5. *Captain Kidd and His Skeleton Island,* as above.

Chapter XI—HUE AND CRY

1. *Documents Relative to the Colonial History of New York.*
2. *Pirate Laureate,* by W. H. Bonner, Rutgers University Press, New Brunswick, N. J., 1937.

3. Dated April 27, 1698. As far as the author can discover, this document has never before been published. H. E. Huntington Collection. EL 9597. Copy, 4 page folio.

4. *Piracy Was a Business*. As above.

5. *Board of Trade, Proprieties, 1699* (Pennsylvania Historical Society).

Chapter XII–WHAT HAPPENED TO CAPTAIN KIDD'S TREASURE?

1. *Captain Kidd and His Skeleton Island*. As above.

2. *Treasure Hunters*, by Robert I. Nesmith and John S. Potter, Jr., Fawcett Book 506, Greenwich, Connecticut, 1961.

3. *Captain Kidd and His Skeleton Island*. As above.

Appendix

Le Golif

Louis Adhémar Timothée Le Golif, author of *Memoirs of a Buccaneer*, styled himself Captain of the Buccaneers. He went by the name of *Borgnefesse*, because of his singular wound. *Borgnefesse* means, literally, in French "One Buttock" or "Half Bottom." He suffered this wound on his first buccaneering expedition with Roc Brasiliano, a noted buccaneer captain. It was during the siege of Granada on the Lake of Nicaragua in front of a little redoubt that the buccaneers were attempting to capture. Le Golif was the first to spring forward when the command to attack was given. At that moment a Spanish cannon ball passed between his legs, rebounded on a rock and carried away all the flesh of his left buttock. Although the wound was quite painful, Le Golif recovered in a month's time, "after which," he wrote, "I became quite nimble again."

Cotton Mather

Cotton Mather, the fiery Congregational minister of Boston, was in his middle thirties during the heyday of the Red Sea Men. He observed, noted and heartily disapproved of their wickedness. Yet, strangely, he had little to denounce in the conduct of the merchants of Boston who were subsidizing the pirates and buying their loot. Nor did he inveigh against the freebooters at this time. It was not until 1723 that he thundered from the pulpit against them, choosing appropriately to make his denunciation immediately following the execution of a parcel of pirates at Newport, Rhode Island. His sermon has a quaint title: "An Essay Upon Remarkables in the Way of Wicked Men."* After thundering against every sort of evil attributable to the pirates, he declared, "Have you not particularly Marked this in the way of the Wicked men? That the Way of Piracy and Robbery, & of the Outrageous Wickedness whereunto the Pirates and Robbers abandon themselves is a Way which the Holy God appears as a Swift Witness against; a Way wherein Sinners bring a Swift Destruction upon themselves . . . Jer.[emiah] 17-11: 'He that getteth Riches and not by Right shall leave them in the midst of his Days and his end shall be a Fool . . .' Hear, hear the cry of the horrible scaffold upon you . . . Among the dolorous Ejaculations of the Dying Pirates, how often do you hear them Confessing . . . Shall this confession make no impression on you?"

Captain Kidd's Commission

William Rex

William the Third, by the grace of God, King of England, Scotland, France and Ireland, Defender of the Faith etc. To our trusty and well beloved Captain William Kid, Commander of the ship *Adventure Galley*, or to any other the commander of the same for the time being, GREETING: WHEREAS we are informed, that Captain Thomas Too

---

* Published in pamphlet form at New London, Conn., 1723.

[Tew], John Ireland, Captain Thomas Wake, and Captain William Maze, or Mace, and other subjects, natives or inhabitants of New York, and elsewhere in our Plantations in America, have associated themselves, with divers others, wicked and ill-disposed persons, and do, against the Law of Nations, commit many and great Piracies, robberies and depredations on the seas upon the parts of America, and in other parts, to the great hindrance and discouragement of trade and navigation, and to the great danger and hurt of our loving subjects, our allies, and all others, navigating the seas upon their lawful occupations, NOW KNOW YE, that we being desirous to prevent the aforesaid mischiefs, and, as much as in us lies, to bring the said Pirates, free booters and sea rovers to justice, have thought fit, and do hereby give and grant to the said William Kid, to whom our Commissioners for exercising the office of Lord High Admiral of England, have granted a commission as a private Man of War bearing the Date the 11th day of December 1695, and unto the Commander of the said ship for the time being, and unto the officers, marines and others, which shall be under your command, full power and authority to apprehend, seize, and take unto your custody as well the said Captain Thomas Too, John Ireland, Captain Thomas Wake, and Captain Maze or Mace, all such Pirates, free booters and sea rovers, being either our subjects, or of other nations associated with them, which you shall meet with upon the seas, or coasts of America, or upon any other seas or coasts, with all their ships and vessels; and all such merchandise, money, goods and wares as shall be found on board, or with them, in case they shall willingly yield themselves. For if they will not yield without fighting, then you are by force to compel them to yield. And we do also require you to bring, or cause to be brought, such Pirates, free booters, or sea rovers, as you shall seize, to a legal trial, to the end that they may be proceeded against according to the Law in such cases. And we do hereby command all our officers, ministers, and our other loving subjects, whatsoever, to be aiding and assisting to you in the premises. And we do hereby enjoin you to keep an exact journal of your proceedings in the execution of the premises, and set down the names of such Pirates, and of their officers and company, and the names of such ships and vessels as you shall, by virtue of these presents take and seize; and the quantities of arms, ammunition, provision and lading of such ships, and the true value of the same, as near as you can judge. And we do hereby strictly charge and command you, as you will answer the contrary to your peril, that you do not, in any manner, offend or molest our friends or allies, their ships or subjects, by colour or pretense of these presents, or the authority thereby granted.

In Witness whereof we have caused our Great Seal of England to be affixed to these presents,

Given at our Court of Kensington, the 26th day of January, 1696, in the seventh year of our reign.

Inventory of Part of Kidd's Loot

A true account of all such gold, silver, jewels and merchandize, late in the posession of Capt. Wm. Kidd, which had been seized and secured by us pursuant to an order from his Excellency, Richard, Earl of Bellamont [sic], bearing date July 7, 1699.

	Ounces
No. 1. One bag of dust, gold	63¾
2. One bag of coined gold, ...	11
and one in silver	124
3. One bag of dust, gold	24¾
4. One bag of silver rings and sundry precious stones	4⅞
5. One bag of unpolished stones	12½

6. One piece crystal, cornelian rings, two
                 agates, two amethysts ... 5
7. One bag of silver buttons and lamps. . 12
8. One bag of broken silver 173½
9. One bag of golden bars 353¼
10. One " " " " 238½
11. One bag of dust, gold 59½
12. One bag of silver bars 309

Samuel Sewall,   Nathl. Byfield   ⎱
Jeremiah Dummer, Andw. Belcher ⎰ Commiss'rs

*The Only True Account of the Dying Speeches
of the Condemn'd Pirates*

The Ordinary of Newgate, his Account of the
Behaviour, Confession and Death of Captain William Kidd and other Pirates, that were executed
yesterday at Execution Dock in Wapping.

On Friday, May 23rd, 1701, these Persons following were
conveyed from Newgate to Execution Dock in Wapping,
by the Officers of the Admiralty, and others carrying the
Silver Oar before them, according to the usual custom. Captain Wm. Kidd born in Scotland, Condemn'd by a High
Court of Admiralty, for the Murther of William Moore,
his Gunner, on the 30th of October 1697, as also for several
piracies and robberies on the high seas, in the East Indies &c.
His behaviour in Newgate after Condemnation, was not so
serious and devout as became a person in his Circumstances;
but whether it proceeded from a Heroick Temper, in not
seeming in any way terrified or afraid at the approaches of
Death (tho' in a violent manner) but being naturally of an
undaunted Mind and Resolution, or from conceited hopes

of obtaining a Pardon, or at least a Reprieve, there being great endeavours (tho' in vain) used for that purpose is yet unknown.

To the last, he would not call the death of Moore "Murther," but esteemed it rather an accidental misfortune, and by reason there was only one blow given and that in passion it provoked him to do so. When he [Moore] was taken prisoner by the Indians, he freely gave £200 for Moore's ransom. All his sailors knew he had always had a great love and respect for Moore.

> (The narrative then describes how John Eldredge was reprieved)

> (Then Lorraine describes how young Darby Mullins, one of Kidd's crew, made a speech at the foot of the gallows, desiring all young men, "but especially Saylors, to take timely warning to avoid Covetousness and all vain and idle company, lest ruin and misery overtake them before they were aware.")

> (Lorraine then returns to Kidd:)

I found (to my unspeakable grief) when he was brought thither [to the gallows] he was inflamed with Drink, which had discomposed his mind, that it was in a very ill frame.

> (Lorraine then describes the cries of Darby Mullins and a French pirate, invoking God and Christ for mercy. Then, almost gloatingly, Lorraine wrote:)

But here I must take notice of a remarkable (I hope most lucky) accident which then happened . . . the Rope with which Capt. Kid was ty'd broke, and so falling to the ground he was taken up alive, and had an opportunity to consider more the Eternity he was lanching [sic] into. He was brought up and again ty'd to the Tree . . . For the last time, I pray'd with him, with a greater satisfaction than I had before that he was penitent.

This is all the account which (in this hurry) can be given of the persons by Paul Lorraine, ordinary, Friday May 23rd, 1701.

Printed for E. Mallet at the Hat and Hawk
in Bridelane

Bibliography

Anonymous, *The History of the Lives and Bloody Exploits of the the Most Noted Pirates*, Hartford, Conn., S. Andrus & Son, 1847. Reprint, New York, N. Y., Empire State Book Co., 1926.

Anonymous, *The Pirates Own Book*. Boston, 1827; reprint, Salem, Mass., Marine Research Society, 1924.

Besson, Maurice, *The Scourge of the Indies*. Translated from the French by Everard Thornton. London, England, G. Routledge & Sons, Ltd., 1929.

Bonner, Willard Hallam, *Pirate Laureate*. New Brunswick, N. J., Rutgers University Press, 1927.

Cochran, Hamilton, *These Are the Virgin Islands*. New York, N.Y., Prentice-Hall, Inc., 1937.

Crump, Helen J., *Colonial Admiralty Jurisdiction in the 17th Century*. London, England, Longmans, Green and Co., 1931.

Dalton, Sir Cornelius, *The Real Captain Kidd: A Vindication*. New York, N. Y., Duffield & Co., 1911.

Dow, George F. and Edmonds, John H., *Pirates of the New England Coast*, 1630-1730. Salem, Mass., Marine Research Society, 1923.

Encyclopedia Britannica, 1911 Edition.

Esquemeling, John (Alexandre Olivier Exquemelin), *The Buccaniers of America*. London, England, Printed for W. Crooke, 1684-85; reprint, London, G. Routledge & Sons, 1925.

Gosse, Philip, *The History of Piracy*, New York, N. Y., Longmans, Green and Co., 1932.

Grey, Charles, *The Merchant Venturers of London*. London, England, H. F. and G. Witherby, 1932.

––– *Pirates of the Eastern Seas*. London, England, S. Low, Marston & Co., Ltd., 1933.

Hamilton, C. J., *The Trade Relations Between England and India, 1600-1896*. Calcutta, India, Thacker, Spink & Co., 1919.

Helm, Thomas, *Treasure Hunting Around the World*. New York, N. Y., Dodd, Mead, 1960.

Hill, Samuel Charles, *Notes on Piracy in Eastern Waters*. Bombay, India, 1923.

Johnson, Captain Charles, *A General History of the Robberies and Murders of the Most Notorious Pirates*. London, England, 1724; reprint, New York, N. Y., Dodd, Mead & Co., 1926.

Kahn, S. H., *The Eastern Trade in the XVIIth Century*. London, England, 1923.

Karraker, Cyrus H., *Piracy Was a Business*. Rindge, N. H., R. R. Smith, 1953.

Labat, Père, *The Memoirs of Père Labat, 1693–1705*. Translated from the French by John Eaden. London, England, Constable & Co., Ltd., 1931.

Leder, Lawrence H., *Robert Livingston's Voyage to New York*. *New York History* (Quarterly) Vol. XXXVI.

Le Golif, Adhémar Timothée, *The Memoirs of a Buccaneer*. Translated from the French by Malcolm Barnes. George Allen & Unwin, Ltd., London, England, 1961.

Miller, Rev. John, *A Description of the Province and City of New York in the Year 1695*. London, England, T. Rodd, 1843.

Monaghan, Frank, *An Examination of the Reputation of Captain Kidd*. *New York History* (Quarterly) Vol. XIV.

Nesmith, Robert I. and Potter, John S., Jr., *Treasure Hunters*. New York, N. Y., Fawcett Publications, 1961.

Oliver, Captain (Samuel) Pasfield (editor), *Madagascar, or Robert Drury's Journal*, *1729*. London, England, T. F. Unwin, 1890.

Ovington, John, *A Voyage to Suratt, in the Year, 1689*. London, England, J. Tonson, 1696; reprint, London, 1929.

Pierce, Arthur D., *Smugglers' Woods*. New Brunswick, N. J., Rutgers University Press, 1960.

Seitz, Don C. (editor), *The Tryal of Captain William Kidd*. New York, N. Y., Printed for R. R. Wilson, Inc., 1936.

Stokes, I. N. Phelps, *Iconography of Manhattan Island*, New York, N. Y., R. H. Dodd, 1915–1928.

Watson, John F., *Annals and Occurrences of New York City and State*. Philadelphia, Pa., 1846.

Wilkins, Harold T., *Captain Kidd and His Skeleton Island*. New York, N. Y., Liveright Publishing Corp., 1937.

——— *Hunting Hidden Treasures*. New York, E. P. Dutton & Co., Inc., 1929.

DOCUMENTARY MATERIALS

Board of Trade Plantations General, Vols. 1689–1702. The Pennsylvania Historical Society, Philadelphia, Pa.

Board of Trade Proprieties (Penna.), *Vols. 1699–1701.* The Pennsylvania Historical Society, Philadelphia, Pa.

Documents Relative to the Colonial History of the State of New York, Vols. I and III. Albany, N. Y., 1853–54.

Historical MSS Commission Reports, Portland MSS IV. London, England, 1932.

Penn's Letter Book, 1699–1703. The Pennsylvania Historical Society, Philadelphia, Pa.

Snead, Robert, *Narrative Relating to a Conversation Between Himself and Gov. Markham [Penna.] About Pyrates. April, 1698.* H. E. Huntington Collection.

Turner, Theophilus, *Deposition Concerning Pirates Sworn Before Gov. Blakiston of Maryland. June, 1699.* H. E. Huntington Collection.

Index